BROKEN TO BE RESTORED
OUR STORY, HIS GLORY

BY: AVRIL SALMON

ASSOCIATE AUTHORS

Copyright © 2025 by Avril Salmon, SPIN Productions Company

All rights reserved. No part of this book may be used or reproduced in any form whatsoever without written permission except in the case of brief quotations in critical articles or reviews.

Printed in the United States of America or Canada

For more information or to book an event, contact:
Email.Spinproduction@yahoo.com

ISBN - Paperback: 978-1-998120-85-7

DEDICATION

This book is dedicated to everyone who has ever experienced being broken and the awesome incredible, redemptive power of restoration. We serve a God who is the best at putting the broken pieces of our hearts back together again. When I was younger and didn't know any better, I believed the nursery rhyme about Humpty Dumpty, when they said that "All the Kings Horses and All the Kings men could NOT put Humpty Dumpty back together again".

I wish I could have introduced Humpty Dumpy to a man called Jesus Christ, the great restorer.

This book is a testimony that no matter how broken some of us were and we thought that there was no way we would EVER be whole again. But God!

To our author Avril Salmon, you were determined that this was the time, no more delays in putting your story out to the world. And, like Peter in the Bible who fished all night and caught nothing, when he listened to Jesus's

BROKEN TO BE RESTORED

SERIES 1

command to throw his net on the other side, he caught an abundance and shared it with others. This is you my sister in Christ. Sharing your abundance with your other SPIN sisters and co-authors, Carol, Christine, Marcia, Carolyn, Mary, Petra and Lorraine. Hats off to you all for putting your story out there in hopes of uplifting and encouraging others. Many of us through the writing process wanted to give up because even though we have been restored or were in the process of restoration, recalling the hurt and trauma to put it on paper was A LOT. But we pushed through the uncomfortable and painful moments to share our stories with all those who will read this book.

This book has been a long time coming. We thank our families and friends, some who had no idea what broke us but were there to help us heal. The ones who were responsible for our brokenness, we thank you because we would not have known the restorative power of God if you

BROKEN TO BE RESTORED

SERIES 1

had not thrown us in the fire, tried to drown us in deep waters, tried to strangle our sense of well being to destroy our mental health. We hope someone, somewhere who reads this book will know that God can put the broken pieces of our lives back together again, better and stronger than it was before; like it was never broken in the first place. Again, I proclaim, What a God!

Written by Carol Johnson

CONTENTS

DEDICATION

FORWARD

1. I'M STILL HERE

By:Avril Salmon

2. THE WOLF

By:Christine Graham-Allen

3. HE IS NOT KILLING YOU; HE IS PERFECTI]

By:Minister Marcia Benjamin

4. A NARROW ESCAPE

By:Mary Joseph

5.BROKEN FOR GOD'S TIMING

By:Lorraine Dawson

6. AFTER HER PASSING

By:Carol Johnson

7. THE POWER OF PAIN

By:Carolyn C. William

8 BROKEN FRAGMENT

By:Petra Mitchell

FORWARD

By Marcia Benjamin MDIV, Registered Psychotherapist (Q)

'Broken to be restored', this book speak volumes to so many areas and places in our lives where dilapidation, destruction, demolition, shame and ridicule can be seen as normative or a part of the mental health spectrum. This is mistaken as part of human construction and so it is inevitable that it will occur at some point in our lives. This treatise is a compilation of the broken fragments from the aftermath of tears, sorrows, brokenness, disappointments, sickness, diseases, abandonment and rejection that these authors have dealt with in their lives.

Through pain, tears and the possibilities of re-catastrophizing themselves, they choose to tell their stories. These women are mothers, sisters, wives, daughters, pastors, prophetesses and whatever status of life they were called to. They

BROKEN TO BE RESTORED

SERIES 1

were not exempt from pain, hurt, shame, rejection or abandonment and yet they told their stories.

I applaud the main author, our "Heroine" Pastor Avril Salmon. She saw the need, felt the pain and decided to help her sisters. She experienced all that her sisters experienced and more and decided that she would champion this cause. She decided to use her skills of networking, advocacy and storytelling to bring about healing, justice, dignity and restoration to her sisters.

I have been given the privilege to be a co-author only due to my nature and designation. I love people and desire that all would prosper and do extremely well in life. As a therapist., I had the awesome pleasure of meeting and developing a therapeutic alliance with Pastor Avril over five years ago. I heard her stories, I saw her tears, I felt her pain. I watched as this "damaged rose" began to bloom again. She began to pollinate and gave life to herself and to so many others.

BROKEN TO BE RESTORED

SERIES 1

She allowed her "broken vessel" to be converted into a vessel of honour and brought glory to her God. I am so honoured to join these beautiful women, as they retell their stories again and again, giving Him all the glory!

CHAPTER 1
I'M STILL HERE

WRITTEN BY: AVRIL SALMON

" Bye, Mama," I remembered saying, as I saw my mother walking towards the plane. As I stood on the deck at the airport, waving goodbye, I wondered if I would ever see Mom again. A thought came into my mind, and I felt a pain in my heart that no little girl my age should have to deal with. " Grandma, where's Mama going?" I asked. " To a better place, to better her life and yours," she replied. As I watched the plane take off in the dark of the night, oh, what pain I felt. This pain was a constant companion that remained with me over the many, many years to come.

BROKEN TO BE RESTORED

SERIES 1

I was only two years old, and the only question I remembered asking repeatedly was, 'Grandma, where's my mama? And when is she coming back?' I would ask that question repeatedly for three years. Each time I saw a plane flying overhead, I would jump up and down in excitement, convinced it was bringing my mom back to me. I looked up for another plane, and then another, and that continued for as long as I could remember, but Mom never came home to me.

Well, as they say, life goes on, and I started to get accustomed to my new life with grandma. After a while, some joy returned to my life, especially because of my Uncle V, who had 'special needs' because he was deaf and dumb, and my baby brother, who was only eight months old, when my mother left. My grandma was a caterer, so every morning I would wake up at 5:00 a.m. to keep her company while she cooked. Grandma was an excellent cook, preparing all types of delicious food that she would take down to the docks to sell to the men for lunch. She was a terrific cook, and even at that tender age, I learned a lot about cooking. No wonder I am an excellent cook now, thanks to Grandma. She did the best she could to take care of my Uncle V, my little brother, and I. Life was very good for those three years, but then the unthinkable happened. It was now Grandma's turn to leave Jamaica, leaving me and Uncle V in the care of my great-grandmother, who I thought

BROKEN TO BE RESTORED

SERIES 1

was a mean, wicked witch. At the time I was only five years old, but I believed God blessed me with a great mind, because I vividly remembered everything that happened, as if it were only yesterday. My great-grandmother, Nana, was not a kind woman. At times, she would shout at me and slap me for no reason. When I came to live with her, she was taking care of a young boy whom I was told was my cousin. I didn't understand this, as he was half Chinese and I was black. He thought he was better than me. He was very handsome. He had light skin with straight black hair and I had dark skin with nappy hair. So many times, he would tell lies that got me into so much trouble. He would beat me because he was older, and then he would tell my Nana that I did all these cruel things to him, which wasn't true. I would end up getting beaten with whatever she could find. Sometimes, I would be punished and go to bed without food or drink because of this mean little boy. My great-grandmother treated him like he was royalty, and I was treated like his maid or a slave. No matter what he did, Nana would turn a blind eye to his cruelty.

Many times, I wish I was old enough to write to my grandmother to let her know what was going on with Uncle V and I.

BROKEN TO BE RESTORED

SERIES 1

Proverbs 13:24 says, 'Do not spare the rod and spoil the child,' and that's exactly what she did with him. Years later, I found out that this young man, my so-called cousin, became a notorious criminal who was wanted by the police for a few years. I was told by my brother a few years after I migrated to Canada, that he was brutally killed by the police. I was told that his body was riddled with bullets. My brother called it 'overkill'.

I often wondered what my great-grandmother would have thought, if she were still alive, to know that she helped shape the way his life went. Had she read the bible, she would have seen that Proverbs 22:6 "train up a child in the way he should go: and when he is old he will not depart from it". During those times, I envied my baby brother, who went to live with my father when grandma left, but I was happy that I was the one who endured that treatment instead of my little brother.
I would rather die than see Nana abuse him. She had no conscience. I would never have traded places with him for her to treat him the way I was treated, especially since he was only a baby. Many times, I likened my living experience to living in hell. I truly thought Nana was related to the devil. Not only was I crying for my mother, but I was also crying for my grandmother because of all the pain I was enduring. I would often ask myself, 'Why would a good God do such a cruel thing to a little girl, by sending away her mother and grandmother at once?' I found out later in life that Jeremiah 29:11 says, "For I know the thoughts

BROKEN TO BE RESTORED

SERIES 1

that I think toward you, saith the LORD, thoughts of peace, and not of evil, to give you an expected end. As I reminisce back on the past, I realized that nothing happened by chance. God has his scribe writing out the plans for each person's life. Romans 8:28 says, "all things work together for good to them that loves God and to those who are called according to his purposes".

So all this time God was working out my life for his good. Now,I can truly say the reason for writing this book is to show how God has turned my test into a beautiful testimony. As I continue to write these books, my readers will come to appreciate how great and wonderful our God is. He has proven that he has been with me through all the storms and trials that I have been through, and he has never left me. He was there all those times when I thought I would fall, he kept me and didn't let go. Psalms 91:11 says, "he will give his angels charge over me, to keep me in all his ways. They will bare me up in their hands so I will not dash my foot against a stone.

Life did not get any better for me, as I continued to live with my great Grandmother. I had to wash all our clothes by hand, we didn't have a washer or dryer, and I had to clean the house and go to the store for her before I left for school. Some days, I don't know how I managed to survive with that lady.

There's a saying, 'God kept me like he kept the fresh fish in the salted water,' and really, he did, because during that time, I should

BROKEN TO BE RESTORED

SERIES 1

have lost my sanity had it not been for my God, "Hallelujah!" Uncle V brought a lot of joy into my heart. We had each other to lean on. With him not having his mother and me not having my mother, our love grew because we had no one who understood our struggle. I remembered praying and genuinely believing that God answered my prayers. I believed that God answered my prayers because I went to live with my father. I was very happy because I was finally reunited with my baby brother, and my older I was only two years old, and my baby brother was eight months old, so I thought of him as my child and loved him with agape love. I was now back with my 'son.' At that time, I didn't know much about my older brother, but it was fun being around him.

Life was not so bad living with dad, except he had a woman living with us, who had a few kids of her own, who were not my father's children, and she treated her kids as princes and princesses, and my brothers, and I like paupers. When my dad wasn't home, she gave her children the best treatment, the best food, everything was best for her kids. My brothers and I had to settle for whatever was left. This went on for quite a while until my father found out about the bad treatment. I cannot recall how he knew, but I thank God he did. That was the end of that miserable treatment. She packed up her kids and everything she had and was gone in the blink of an eye.

BROKEN TO BE RESTORED

SERIES 1

Well, dad settled into his new position as both mom and dad. Even though I was young, I was a real little housewife. I could cook because my grandmother taught me well. I could cook up a five-course meal. I could clean and was. I could do almost anything a grown-up could do. My dad was very sick, he had chronic asthma, so I had to keep everything neat and very clean. Everything had to be dust-free. I was quite the little housewife. Taking care of my dad and two brothers, I didn't feel like a slave anymore, and I didn't feel hopeless at all. Life was a lot better.

My Uncle V would come by very often to see us. We had so much fun with him, even though he couldn't hear or speak. He wasn't convinced that he couldn't; most evenings after work, you could find my uncle on the street corner singing all sorts of songs. He could feel the beat and hum to the tune. Everybody knew what he was singing because he hummed to the beat, even though he couldn't hear. He would sing the latest hits of the '60s and hum he did! I wish I could imitate his actions for you right now. You would just laugh when you see how he did it. He was 'Michael Jackson' of his era. He was also the best dancer in town. I believe if he could talk, he might have become a millionaire, because he certainly got a lot of money for entertaining the crowd.

BROKEN TO BE RESTORED

SERIES 1

Uncle V was a very wonderful uncle. When I was much smaller, I thought he was crossing his eyes, so we could laugh, not realizing that was how he was born. But he was the joy of my life. I realized later in life that you don't have to say, "I love you." He never said it to me, but I have yet to see someone who possessed the love that he showed to me and my little brother. Many evenings, he would come for me to give him something good to eat, because my food reminded him of his mother's cooking. She taught me well. His mother, my grandmother, was a great cook. Even though I was only about nine years old, I could cook almost anything.

I know Uncle V was very sad. He was writing on paper, asking, "Where was his mom?" There's a saying, "Like mother, like daughter," because my mother left me, and his mother left him—no letters, no phone call, no mother. He often wrote, asking where his mother was, and I didn't know what to say. The story goes on. Uncle V was getting the same bad treatment from his grandmother, who was my great-grandmother. Many times, he would come to my home crying; he was hungry, she wasn't feeding him, he was skinny, and he was losing weight. How helpless I felt! I could only give him some food. Where was the address for Grandma, so I could write to her to let her know that I was not with her mom any longer, and the disadvantage that was taken of her baby boy? Well, not a boy any longer but a grown man, they say the leaf does not fall far from the tree.

BROKEN TO BE RESTORED

SERIES 1

When I got older, I learned a lot about generational curses and why people do the things they do without even understanding why. The concept of sin that is passed down from generation to generation varies. Exodus states that God visits the iniquity of the Father on the children to the third and fourth generation.

I will never forget the evening we were home, and a voice came screaming through the gate, saying, "It's Uncle V! It's Uncle V! He's dead!" At first, I thought this must be a joke. Angels do not die! This must be a nightmare. Well, my nightmare became a reality when I ran to Nana's house and saw my Uncle V's body lying dead on the cold floor. With my voice of anguish, I shouted with the loudest voice, "Who did this to my uncle?" Silence rushed across the crowded yard; no one made a sound. My head was pumping and my mind was spinning, "Someone is going to pay!" I said, "Who did this to my uncle? What happened?" Still, no one said a word. Through a crack in the crowd, I saw my grandmother sitting. She was sitting on the bench. I'm not sure how it happened, but in what seemed like a flash, I was standing in front of her. "What happened to my uncle?" I shouted.

She muttered, "He came home from work. I was cooking. Maybe he was hungry, and he started to go into my pot. I took his hands away. He pushed me. I pushed him in his chest, and he fell." I knew she was lying. I knew she hit him so hard in his chest, and that must

BROKEN TO BE RESTORED

SERIES 1

have caused him to have a heart attack. He was such a gentle soul; he
wouldn't hurt a fly. Gone. Gone too soon at the hands of this wicked old lady. And the worst part of it? Nothing came out of it. Police could not charge her because there was no evidence, no eyewitness to convey what happened. Many, many people came to his funeral to mourn this wonderful man. At the time, I didn't know much about God, but one thing was for sure: he was gone to be with his Maker and join the choir of Heaven, singing praises to the God of Israel.

Even though this was a sad event, I was anxious because after many years, I was about to see my grandmother, his mother, and most of all, my mother at Uncle V's funeral. My brothers and I anticipated seeing her again. My little brother was now six years old and could not wait to see the woman he had never met. We could not sleep. We did not sleep for many nights, just waiting for that moment when I would see my mother. But as time drew close for the funeral, to our surprise, Grandma and my mom never came, and the devastation formed all over again. "How could this be?" I asked God. "Why do bad things always happen to good people?" I pondered this question for many months after, and I cried day and night. I could not believe anyone could be so heartless. "Bye, Uncle V. I know I will see you one day." As I write this book, not only am I a born-again woman of God, but I am an ordained pastor, knowing that one day I will

BROKEN TO BE RESTORED

SERIES 1

see my Uncle V again in glory.

After the funeral, neither my brothers nor I ever spoke about my mom again. We learned to mask the pain and move on. Later in life, I came across a chapter in the Bible, in Psalms 68:5, which says, "God is a father to the fatherless." And because there's no gender in God, I'm sure He is a mother to the motherless. My dad continued to do the best he could for the three of us, even though it was a struggle. He had some help from his sister, who lived in the States at the time. She would often send barrels to Jamaica with food, clothes, and different things to help us out. We had one aunt in Jamaica, who was my father's sister. She would often cook some food or wash clothes for us, but I was the little mother for my family. My dad was a good father; he worked very hard to support us.
My father had chronic asthma, which, when he had an attack, would be so severe. Repeatedly, I thought we would lose him, but God knew we needed him. Many times, the back of his foot would break out into sores and crack from top to bottom. He would be in excruciating pain. I would feel so sad for him. I would bathe his feet. I would do anything that I could to comfort my dad until he was better.

My dad had an addiction: he was a hard marijuana smoker. My father was also very abusive; he often beat

BROKEN TO BE RESTORED

SERIES 1

us. I do not understand how a father who was supposed to love and protect his children would use a piece of a car tire, around 30 inches long, to discipline us. Reminiscing back, I wondered if my dad lived in Canada, he would have been in prison for being abusive to his children. My dad would roll a marijuana spliff and give it to us, and he thought that was ok. Looking back now that I'm older, I really believed that my father was mentally challenged.

What in the name of God could he have been thinking of? I hated smoking these marijuana joints [spliffs], as he would call them, but until this day, my siblings are chronic smokers because of my father. My brothers and sisters liked to be high; they didn't like to go to school. I believe my father smoked so much that he lost a few screws from his brain. How else can you describe his behavior? He didn't find anything wrong with smoking and getting high. When he was high on his weed, he would give us something to do, and sometimes we forgot because we were so high then he forgot, or maybe we forgot because we were so high, and that would make him beat the living daylights out of us. Thank you, Lord, for your saving grace.

My father was always high, and we lived in a place called a 'tenement yard', where there were at least 100 families. My father would invite his friends to come over, and they were always high, so my father never got the chance to see what was happening to me.

BROKEN TO BE RESTORED

SERIES 1

He never saw what his friends were doing to me, his little daughter. I'm sure he wasn't turning a blind eye; he was just very illiterate about the fact that his friends were molesting me, right in front of him, and he didn't see. I wanted to tell him many times that Mr. Mike (not his real name) was touching me, but if Mr. Mike said that was a lie, I would get a beating from my father. When his friend came over and asked, "Where's your daughter?" my father would call me, and if I tried to hide, he would slap me for
hiding. I was just hiding because I could not stand the pain of what his fingers were doing to me. He would often bring me candies and treats that I didn't want because I would be in too much pain to even eat them. What a price I had to pay for not having my mom to protect me from these evil demons from hell! I vividly remembered one day my father was as close to Mr. Mike, and I swore my father would have seen what he was doing, but he was too high to even look that way. God, why? I hated them. I was molested over and over again.

But it was such a blessing when my aunt, who lived in America, was told by her doctor that she had to come home to Jamaica, because she was blind in one eye and going blind in the other, and that was the blessing I was looking forward to. We eventually moved to a beautiful home, away from the slums, away from his friends, and away from all the hurt and pain. God knew I've had

BROKEN TO BE RESTORED

SERIES 1

enough. My father's friends never came to visit him in our new home. God be praised. We now had our own beds and were comfortable and happy. Well, my joy was short-lived. My aunt did come home, but I'll tell you this: the Bible declares in John 10:10, "The thief comes only to steal and kill and destroy." That was the enemy's plan for my life: to take me out. But a latter part of that text declares, "God came to give life and to give it more abundantly."

After my aunt came to Jamaica, she needed someone to take her frustration out on. After all, she had to leave everything in the USA with her husband, her friends, her home, everything. She had so much and so, she was so angry. She was very angry that she decided I was the one she was going to take out her frustration on. I'll tell you the reason she chose me. When I was three years old, she came to visit Jamaica to see my father. She came to my grandmother's home to see my little brother and me. What I found out was that she thought I was so beautiful, she wanted to take me for a few weeks, and she would have remained in Jamaica. I was only three years old, had just lost my mom, and I didn't know this lady, so I didn't want to go with her. What she told me was, "I knew you were no good. I knew you were wicked." How? How could she say such a thing? I was only three years old, but she summed me up in her mind that I was wicked, because I did not want to go with her.

BROKEN TO BE RESTORED

SERIES 1

She hated me because I didn't go with her.
Now I'm living in her home, and if you think my great-grandmother was bad, or my grandmother, or even my mother, they were nothing compared to the hell I would have faced for the next few years of my life. As I said, my father did work hard to make ends meet.

When he had to pay rent, it was hard. However, now he was living with his sister and did not have to pay a cent. My dad was good, but did not like responsibility, so my aunt found a way to make me pay by lying so many times. She would have caused my father to beat the living daylights out of me because she would say, "Get out," and my father did not like responsibility, so he would rather listen and abuse me. Several times, I could have died because of her. I got a huge cut on my leg that could have killed me; I had 58 stitches on the inside and 48 on the outside. Only God kept me. I was like a chick under His wing.

Whatever we go through in life, God wrote the script for our lives; He watches over us.

There's a song that says, "God will turn your test into a testimony, and He will teach you that your trials are only blessings in disguise. He will pull up all your values with the fragrance of the lilies, and one day I will testify, 'Thank you, Jesus, for keeping care of me and your tender mercies.'" I went through many horrible things, but God took me through them.

BROKEN TO BE RESTORED

SERIES 1

He overshadowed me and kept me from all harm and danger. I remembered one night; I was locked out. I was so scared. I was only about 11 at this time. My aunt told my dad I did something so terrible that he wanted to kill me, but God knows I did not. So, I was locked outdoors. I was so tired of being beaten because I didn't do what she said I did. Many times, I would always end up in my room where I would be beaten mercilessly, and my older brothers and sisters would just leave and go to their friends' houses. The other two were her prince and princesses, so after I got the beating, she would call them to come into her room. Mighty God, I remember one night I was outside, and there was this man in the community whom everyone was afraid of.

They called him Bad Rasta. He saw me, jumped over the fence, and held onto me, and he wanted to rape me, and if he did, he would have killed me. But God—how did He let me go and leave? It had to be God's grace and mercy.

I took the time to tell and retell my story. I have many more stories of abuse, abandonment, rejection, but through it all, my 'Champion and Saviour' carried me through all the storms and trials of my life.

Today, I am alive to tell the stories, today I am an ordained pastor, community advocate, intercessor, author, and leader. God has given me beauty for ashes and the oil of joy for the mourning that I endured. I am here to convince you my sister or brother, that whoever puts their trust in Jesus Christ, will never fail or be forsaken, Indeed, I am still here,

because of the "I am".

BROKEN TO BE RESTORED

SERIES 1

Dear Parents,

Can I speak to you from a place of The Word of God, which tells us that "Children are a gift from the Lord, they are a reward from him" Psalms 127:3. With these words, I want to caution you about the people you let into your sphere of influence or your circle. In the book of Jeremiah 17:9, it tells us that the heart is deceitful above all things, who can understand it. Meaning a man may never know what's in his heart until he is faced with temptation. This is the reason why many people find it unbelievable when an upstanding person is accused of a hideous crime. Most people are fooled because they look at the outward appearance.

In that case, that gift (your child/children) must be handled with care; they must be protected from the enemy.

You must not be ignorant of the devil's devices. Be aware of the wolves. (evil people) It doesn't matter how well you think you know them; it could be the closest person to you. Be very careful. Remember when situations happen, there is always a high price to pay; physical, mental, psychological, scars that will be left on your child for the rest of their lives, and sometimes this could trickle down to your grandchildren and great-grandchildren. Sometimes this can be caused by negligence but sometimes it's pure innocent on your part and because of this a doorway in the spiritual Realm can be opened and here comes a curse that down to the

BROKEN TO BE RESTORED

SERIES 1

Third and fourth generation and if there is no one rises up to break that curse it will go down to a thousand generation this is the fact please I'm imploring you do not leave your children to chance many times your friends your family even your husband whether the kids are his or not they wil do unimaginary things to these innocent children they sometimes even threaten the kids if you talk I'll kill your mom or kill your sisters kill your brothers and there comes a mental and psychological scars for me I've been through a lot and I'm imploring you do not let your children go through what I went through when you read my book through and through you will see the things I had to endure your and there are things that I didn't say that I will say in my next book I encourage you to speak to your children tell him not to be afraid educate them about things that these culprit. Might say to them so they will not talk because of fear tell them not to believe the lies of whomever it is that tell them. Train your children in the arts of spiritual warfare; they are never too young to learn the skill to pray, and teach them about the blood of Jesus Christ of Nazareth. I pray that God will give you the wisdom on how to protect them.

CHAPTER 2
THE WOLF

WRITTEN BY: AMB.CHRISTINE GRAHAM-ALLEN

Sally was seven years old when she first heard the growl. It wasn't a loud sound, not like the howling wolves in picture books or movies. No, this was quieter. Slippery. It hissed its way into her life through whispers, sideways glances, and a betrayal so deep, it split the path of her life in two.

She was just a little girl, an immigrant child from the Caribbean trying to find her place in a new land. The air was different here. The colors are colder. The laughter is more distant. And yet, Sally, full of innocent hope, still believed she could belong.

BROKEN TO BE RESTORED

SERIES 1

The betrayal came from someone close. A family member she trusted. A grown-up who should have protected her. Instead, they pointed a finger and told a lie — a lie that turned her world upside down. And just like that, Sally was marked. Labeled. Silenced.

When Sally tried to defend herself, they said she was being disrespectful. When she cried, they said she was too sensitive. So she learned to hold it in. To nod. To obey. To please. That's how she survived.

She didn't know it then, but that was the first time she met the wolf — not in fur and fangs, but in shame and silence. The wolf wasn't a beast hiding in the woods. It was a spirit. A presence. It crouched behind the smiles of adults who used religion as a weapon. It lurked in the corners of classrooms where teachers ignored her. It fed on her silence, growing stronger every time she bit her tongue.

Sally began to chase approval like breadcrumbs in the forest, hoping it would lead her home. She became the helper, the fixer, the overachiever. But no matter how much she did, it was never enough. She felt unseen, unheard, and unbelieved.

BROKEN TO BE RESTORED

SERIES 1

She wanted to believe that if she were just good enough, obedient enough, helpful enough, then maybe they would love her, maybe she would belong.

And that created a blind spot… and then… here comes the wolf. Every time there's a blind spot like that, it's an open door for the wolf.

She didn't know that trying to be good to gain acceptance was a door. A silent door swinging wide open. But Sally's story doesn't end there. At 55 years old, through every storm and scar, she's learning to build her life on the Rock. Like the third little lamb — the one who listened to the voice of the Shepherd — she's no longer building her house on fear, performance, or approval. She's building on Christ, the only foundation strong enough to withstand the wolf.

Sally is no longer just surviving. She's learning to recognize the wolf — even when it shows up in sheep's clothing — and tune her ears to the true Shepherd's voice. The voice that says she is loved, protected, and chosen.

If you're brave enough to face the wolf in your own life — and ready to learn how to hear the Shepherd's voice — then turn the page.

BROKEN TO BE RESTORED

SERIES 1

1. Recognizing the Wolf: Identifying the Subtle Attack

Scripture Focus:

"Beware of false prophets, which come to you in sheep's clothing, but inwardly they are ravening wolves." – Matthew 7:15 (KJV)

Jesus warned us that wolves rarely present themselves as threats. They look safe, familiar, even comforting. They speak your language. They might smile at you, tell you what you want to hear, and even seem to care about your best interests. But inwardly, their motives are destructive.

The wolf isn't always a person. Sometimes, the wolf is a spirit of deception—a voice whispering lies into your thoughts. Sometimes it's a toxic belief system you inherited from childhood. Other times it's a relationship, a workplace culture, or a manipulative leader who drains your soul while pretending to care.

Signs You've Been Bitten

1. You strive for approval. You overextend yourself, overcompensate, and take on roles that aren't even yours, hoping someone will finally notice you.

BROKEN TO BE RESTORED

SERIES 1

2. Your self-worth is tied to performance. You believeyou're only as valuable as your last accomplishment.

3. You silence your voice. You minimize your needs,your opinions, and your feelings because you don't want to upset anyone.

4. You fear rejection constantly. Your decisions are shaped by whether or not people will accept you.

Reflection Question:

Do any of these patterns show up in your life? Which one is the loudest right now?

These are not random struggles. They are signs that you have been bitten. The wolf leaves venom that works its way into your subconscious, shaping how you think, act, and see yourself.

And here's the dangerous part: a blind spot becomes a doorway. When you believe, "I must be perfect to be loved," or "If I don't help, I don't matter," you've left a silent door swinging wide open.

BROKEN TO BE RESTORED

SERIES 1

2. Breaking the Pattern: Closing the Door on the Wolf

Scripture Focus:

"But all things that are reproved are made manifest by the light: for whatsoever doth make manifest is light." – Ephesians 5:13 (KJV)

The good news is this: the bite is not the end of the story. You can heal. You can close the door. But it won't happen by accident.

Shining Light on the Blind Spots

The first step is awareness. You must allow the Holy Spirit to reveal the lies you have believed about yourself.

Ask yourself:

- Why do I feel the need to overcompensate?
- What am I afraid will happen if I say no?
- What lies have I believed about my worth?

Journaling these questions can be powerful. Writing helps bring what's hidden in your subconscious into the light where it can be addressed.

BROKEN TO BE RESTORED

SERIES 1

Detaching Identity from Performance

The wolf wants you to believe that your worth is tied to what you do. But the Word of God says otherwise:

Scripture Focus:

"For by grace are ye saved through faith; and that not of yourselves: it is the gift of God: Not of works, lest any man should boast." – Ephesians 2:8–9 (KJV)

> Your identity is not rooted in your ability to meet others' expectations; it is rooted in Christ alone.
>
> Declare these truths:
>
> - I am loved apart from my performance (Romans 5:8).
>
> - I am chosen and accepted (Ephesians 1:4–6).
>
> - I do not have to earn God's love; I already have it.

BROKEN TO BE RESTORED

SERIES 1

This shift won't feel natural at first because the wolf's venom has trained you to seek approval. But as you repeatedly replace lies with truth, your mind begins to heal (Romans 12:2).

Establishing Boundaries

Wolves thrive in environments without boundaries.

Scripture Focus:

"Keep thy heart with all diligence; for out of it are the issues of life." – Proverbs 4:23 (KJV)

Boundaries are not about pushing people away; they are about protecting what God has entrusted to you.

Ask yourself:

- Which relationships consistently drain me?
- Where do I say "yes" out of guilt rather than calling?
- What boundaries has God been prompting me to set but I've ignored?

BROKEN TO BE RESTORED

SERIES 1

Healing the Bite

Once you have identified the wound and closed the door, you must allow God to heal the bite. This is where forgiveness becomes crucial.

Scripture Focus:

"For if ye forgive men their trespasses, your heavenly Father will also forgive you." – Matthew 6:14 (KJV)

Forgiveness is not saying what the wolf did was okay. It is releasing the grip of bitterness from your heart so you can be free.

Prayer:

Father, I choose to forgive (name). I release them into Your hands. Heal my heart where I have been bitten.

3. Rebuilding with a New Mindset: Living Wolf-Free
Scripture Focus:

"Behold, I give unto you power to tread on serpents and scorpions, and over all the power of the enemy: and nothing shall by any means hurt you." – Luke 10:19 (KJV)

BROKEN TO BE RESTORED

SERIES 1

Strengthening Discernment

Hebrews 5:14 says those who are mature have trained themselves to discern good and evil. Discernment is not suspicion; it is the ability to see beyond appearances.

Pray for discernment:

Lord, help me see people and situations through Your eyes. Expose the wolves. Reveal motives. Keep me sensitive to Your Spirit.

The Holy Spirit will often nudge you with a sense of unrest when something is off. Don't dismiss those checks in your spirit.

Finding Healthy Community

Healing accelerates when you are surrounded by safe, godly people.

Look for a community where:

- You are valued, not used.

- Truth is spoken in love, not manipulation.

- There is mutual accountability and encouragement.

Living from Fullness

The wolf preys on emptiness. When you live from a place of deficit—hungry for approval, desperate for belonging—you are vulnerable. But when you live from the fullness of God's love, the wolf has nothing to explore.

Spend time in His presence daily. Worship. Pray. Read the Word. When your heart is full, you stop looking to people to validate you.

Walking in Confidence

Finally, remember that you are not helpless.
Declare aloud:
- I have authority in Christ to resist the wolf (Luke 10:19).

- I will not be devoured by fear, rejection, or manipulation.

- I walk in freedom because Christ lives in me.

BROKEN TO BE RESTORED

SERIES 1

Visualize

Imagine living without the constant pressure to prove yourself. Imagine being able to say "no" without guilt, to

love without fear, to walk in rooms fully confident in who God made you to be.

That life is possible. That's the wolf-free life.

It's not that wolves will never show up again. They will. But now you recognize the masks. You see the open doors before they swing wide. You guard your heart, close the door, and walk in the authority Jesus gave you.

Sally's story doesn't have to be yours. You don't have to chase breadcrumbs through the forest anymore.

You are already home.

You belong.

You are loved—not because of what you do, but because of who you are.

And when the wolf comes knocking, you'll be ready.

BROKEN TO BE RESTORED

SERIES 1

Reflection & Response

1. Where do you see evidence of "the wolf's bite" in your life?

2. What lie have you believed about your worth that God wants to replace with His truth?

3. What boundary do you need to set this week to guard your heart?

Congratulations! You made it through this chapter without allowing life's distractions to pull you away. That alone is a victory worth celebrating. Finishing what you start is always a step in the right direction, and today, you have done just that.

Sally's story is not just Sally's story. There are countless "Sallys" all over the world, in every shape, size, colour, and creed. Pain and striving know no boundaries. There is no colour to the human heart, no barriers in its language. Hurt speaks to hurt, and healing speaks to healing.

By completing this chapter, you have chosen healing. You have chosen to see differently, to rise above the lies, and to reclaim your God-given identity.

BROKEN TO BE RESTORED

SERIES 1

That is no small decision, and I celebrate you for it.
I encourage you to read this chapter again and again. Let the truths sink deep into your spirit. And please, don't keep it to yourself. There is someone you know who desperately needs to read Sally's story and see hope for their own. Share this book with them. Pass the encouragement forward.
Every time we share light, the darkness loses ground. Every time we speak the truth, the wolf loses power. You are part of that chain now—a carrier of hope.

Well done, you have taken an incredible step toward restoration, and I hope you continue to uncover the treasures within you, so that you will appreciate the brokenness that led to your restoration. Thank you.
To God be Glory

BROKEN TO BE RESTORED

SERIES 1

The Wolf

Dear Reader,

Please say this prayer with me before reading this chapter.

"Father, thank You for opening my eyes to the wolves in my life and the lies I've believed... Fill me with Your love so I no longer live in deficit, but in the fullness of Christ. Amen."

With love,

Christine Graham-Allen

Amb., Chrisitne Graham-Allen

BROKEN TO BE RESTORED

SERIES 1

CHAPTER 3
HE IS NOT KILLING YOU; HE IS JUST PERFECTING YOU

WRITTEN BY: MINISTER BENJAMIN

We have read many scriptures which echoes God's perfection. "God will perfect that which concerns you". While that is great, because we must all attain to God's perfection, as it pertains to His qualification for perfection, but do we, as a people understand God's ingredients for perfection?

BROKEN TO BE RESTORED

SERIES 1

Do we understand what is involved in attaining to God's perfection? The scriptures also stated that "You must be holy as I am holy". Does anyone know how to attain holiness or perfection? Doesn't the scriptures emphatically stated that we were born in sin and shaped in iniquity and that all our righteousness is like filthy rags before a holy God? So how does one become holy?

As I attempt to embark on this treatise to gain clarity, wisdom, and understanding, I invite my readers to journey with me, to gain understanding of the mind of our heavenly Father and His perfect love for his creation. My topic may sound paradoxical and a bit deceptive, but the essence of God's truth is the nature of His character. We are from God; we all hold a part of his imagination. We were in His thoughts before we became his reality and so, it makes sense that everything about the human species should be perfect, because our creator was perfect.

So where am I going with this treatise? I am perplexed, confused and utterly frustrated about my Christian Walk at times.

I love God and I believe with my whole being that all Christians love God and do want to please God and make heaven our final abode. We want to escape hell and leave this miserable life of sickness, pain, poverty and all the things that plague us as Christians. Our generations have suffered and suffered and now we get the privilege of being born again and so it's only fitting to believe that our new life with Jesus Christ, our Lord is filled with blessings, glory, goodness, peace and happiness.

BROKEN TO BE RESTORED

SERIES 1

At least that's what I expected when I accepted Jesus Christ as my Lord.

Unfortunately, no one told us about the aftermath of our salvation. No one shared that all hell breaks loose when you try to break free from hell's grasp on your life. You see, we were utterly deceived. While we were busy in the world living and doing things "my or our way" we were on Satan's agenda. We are in the world and serving the devil. He was no threat to us because we were living, loving, carousing, fornicating, lying, stealing and doing things his way, so we were all good. We pleased him and we were his henchmen and women. We were not bound to convictions, we didn't have to speak truth, we robbed, drank alcohol, took drugs, and did whatever pleased us. We were also oblivious to the fact that we were living on borrowed time.

We were not tempted to serve God; no one bothered us, we were just living our best lives on borrowed time, until God said it's time to come home, and then He placed a brother or sister in our path to show us the way of life. We then start feeling different. We don't understand that transformation has begun, and we are now being translated from the kingdom of darkness, where everything was good to now being transformed into the kingdom of light. We find ourselves being aware of ourselves. We are constantly feeling convicted, guilty, ashamed, sorry and afraid. We are now displaying reverence for God, his house and his people.

BROKEN TO BE RESTORED

SERIES 1

We change our speech, our attitudes, and our behaviours. We are now mindful of our speech and attitude towards others. We are being transformed every day. We desire God's presence more each day, until we finally take the plunge to surrender all to Jesus Christ by giving our lives to him, and then get baptized. It's now official, we have a wedding sermon, and the world now knows that I am a Christian.

This is wonderful, this is an amazing experience for every believer, but no one truly talks about the aftermath. The days when the devil and his demons come to take revenge. When they plot and stalk your life. No one talks about learning to move from being a baby in the Lord and all the attacks that one will encounter. Who talks about losing your job, or when your entire house turns against you? Does someone share when you can't find money to buy your bus ticket, and you wonder where is God?

What happens when sickness clings to your bones and refuses to let you go? How about when a whirlwind that gives you no warning shows up and wipes you out clean? You are left bankrupt, sick with no job. What happens when you lose your six-figure income job and start working mediocre jobs? You see nobody warns you or gives you a sneak preview about this side of your salvation. If you don't believe me, check out the book of Job. The bible explicitly describes this man as the most righteous man in the east. Job was so righteous that he atoned for his children before they even sinned.

BROKEN TO BE RESTORED

SERIES 1

Job did not wait for the poor to come to him, he would go search for those who had nothing, the fatherless,

the widows and the poor. Job was a blessed man until calamity came upon Job. The bible says that there was a day when the sons of God came before Him and Satan also showed up. God asked Satan "have you considered my servant Job? There is none like him in all the earth. He shuns evil and does only what is right". Satan replied, "of course, you have blessed the work of his hands and have built an edge of protection around him but remove the edge of protection and he will curse you to your face (Job 1).

God then gave permission for Satan to touch Job's children, houses, animals, servants and all that Job had. Job had no clue what was taking place in the heavens. It was great that God was bragging and boasting about Job's loyalty and faith. This is the part of my treatise that I questioned God. I admit that we are finite beings *and have no right to ask or tell God anything, but couldn't God give Job a little warning?* We are God's creation, and He alone is God and has every right to do and say whatever He pleases. We see Job's saga continued to the point that Satan was given the permission to touch Job's body. The bible said that Job was unrecognizable. The bible describes Job's body that he was covered in maggots to the point that he was unrecognizable. His wife couldn't stand the sight of her husband, that she

BROKEN TO BE RESTORED

SERIES 1

encouraged him to curse God and die. His friends came to visit and comfort him, but Satan found a loophole to use them to accuse Job, all the while God remained silent. Now the bible never indicated how long Job's suffering lasted but there was a time when Job's suffering ended, and God restored Job. Everything that was lost was restored and he was doubled blessed. The bible also told us that Job lived a long and blessed life.

Why Must I Suffer To Attain Perfection?

Isaiah 53:3 said He (Jesus) was despised and rejected by mankind, a man of suffering and familiar with pain. Like one from whom people hide their faces, he was despised, and we held him stricken by God. Jesus our saviour was acquainted with grief, he was rejected, and he suffered at the hands of the people whom he came to earth to save. We also knew that all these things were done by Satan, and he used all the same people whom he came to save. God did not spare Jesus from persecution, pain, atrocities, ridicule, suffering, shame
and disgrace. The bible said that if we are going to reign with Jesus, we will have to suffer with him. All throughout the bible, we read about the suffering of Jesus from the time he entered the earth up to the time that he departed the earth. He never lied that we who are called for this life of sanctification will go through tribulation and many harsh sufferings. He promised that he would make a way of escape so that we might be able to bear the persecution.

BROKEN TO BE RESTORED

SERIES 1

The bible did not give us a manuscript about our salvation. We were told that the "Just should live by faith". We were not given any warnings or a telegram as to when our persecution or temptation would come, it just comes and whatever the duration, we are expected to endure it until Jesus makes a way for us to overcome. What we need to know is what is the purpose of this temptation. We need to ask God, what is this lesson about? What are you perfecting in me?

Most times our trials are sent to perfect the areas where we are lacking. Let's say I have a bad temper; God will continue to send me tests and trials until I realize what he is teaching me and use those lessons to get rid of my anger. As soon as I overcome it, I know that another lesson is waiting.

My Own Journey Of Testing And Trials

My own journey started in September 1996, I was 27 years old, and I had migrated from Jamaica only seven years before. I was so ready to live my best life, have fun and eventually meet a guy who I could settle down with. I was in the prime of my life. We started getting the pull and people started telling me about Jesus.

I had such a reverential fear of Jesus that I wouldn't tell someone no when they invited me to church and I would be so afraid to lie. I eventually accepted the call and gave my life to Jesus.

BROKEN TO BE RESTORED

SERIES 1

I had no clue about what I had signed up for. My boyfriend at the time decided to follow me and accepted Jesus Christ.

We were separated from the rest of our family and spent the next four years just learning about Jesus, the bible, the church and Christian living. We lost many of our friends and family because we were not doing the same old things that the world was doing so we were somewhat ostracized. As we started growing in the things of the Lord, so the satanic attacks increased.

I was constantly attacked with sickness, financial struggles, and witchcraft. I also noticed that each time that God declared a prophetic word over my life the enemy would send a counterfeit to shatter it. I was told in January 1996 that I would get pregnant. I was pregnant the next year at the exact time. The prophetic word came through but that year I went to Jamaica and almost lost my life. I came back to Toronto and was in the hospital two days after.

My blood pressure was 220/120 by the time I got to the hospital and was climbing. They had air ambulance take me to Toronto General Hospital to better care for me. I was placed ICU for eight days and had to be placed under a respirator as they had to induce a coma to get my blood pressure down. When I woke up, I could only give God praise and glory. The baby had passed out on the bed, as my body expelled the fetus.

BROKEN TO BE RESTORED

SERIES 1

When I was awakened, I suffered renal failure, heart and lungs failure. My brain was swollen and everything that could go wrong went wrong. After that episode we attempted to get pregnant again, but we lost our babies. We lost six children.

My last pregnancy was Jan 2003, and I thought surely, God will show us mercy. When I went to see the doctor, I was told that the baby had died, and we don't know how long the baby had been dead. This pregnancy really hit me hard. I told the doctor that I was going home. I didn't care how long the baby died; I was so sad and disheartened. I gave up on God, all I kept hearing Satan say where was, your God can't give you one child.? My sister came and picked me up at the clinic, and she said do not to go home.

Come and stay by my place. I remember my sister kept saying please believe in God, don't give up your faith, please sis, keep trusting God. I couldn't. I was crushed, broken, dejected, rejected and disappointed. Satan kept taunting me where is your God and why can't he give you a child?. This was my sixth pregnancy. I was tired. I summed up the courage to go into a fast. I needed to hear God speak to me, why couldn't I get a baby? About the fourth day of the fast about 4am, I heard the Lord speak to me. He said what are you doing? Before I could answer him, he showed me a vision and said you should have died this day. Again, before I could answer, he showed another vision and said you should have died this day and the last vision

BROKEN TO BE RESTORED

SERIES 1

he showed me he said you should have died this day. This really got my attention and the question was who wanted me dead and why was I still alive? I was scared, shocked and shaken. I repented for tempting God and I made a vow to God. I said God forgive me and I repented, and I said God I will never come back to you regarding a child. With or without children, I will serve you until the day you call me home. That day my womb was closed, and I never got pregnant again. I went into the hospital in 2018 and had a total hysterectomy.

God's Ways Are Far Better Than Mine

After I got better, my husband decided to adopt so we started fostering in 2009. We had over twenty (20) children pass through our home. I started loving the children, but they would only stay for two to three weeks at a time. Finally, we got a sibling set, a brother and a sister and they stayed for eleven (11) months. Just as I was getting comfortable saying yes to adopt them the mother started giving me a hard time. I remember the social worker saying to Marcia you need a break. In October 2010, we had a call from the social worker who introduced us to our 3 daughters, Richelle, Nicole and Julie. The social worker said these little girls have no issues; their parents just can't take care of them do you want them? I screamed so hard. This was the beginning of another scary saga.

BROKEN TO BE RESTORED

SERIES 1

All three girls were born positive with drugs in their system. They had all the signs of children who were abused and had all kinds of disabilities. Through it all God kept us, and we did the mandatories, therapy sessions weekly, assessments, doctor's visits, and psychologist assessments. My life was running from appointment to appointment. I was in their seventh home.

Finally, my daughters settled, we adopted them in 2013, and this became their forever home. I stopped fostering and gave all my attention to my children, Richelle was 7, Nicole was 5 and Julie was 3. My girls attended private Christian elementary and then a private Christian high school. We were sharing my life story with the girls one day and God allowed me to hear something so profound. This has helped me to stop trying to figure out the ways in which God works because no one knows His ways except him.

I told the girls that my last pregnancy was in January 2003, and Richelle said, Mom, I was born in November 2003. Then I said two years later we applied for their brother from Cameroon, then Nicole said, Mom, I was born August 2005. I then said two years later, your brother arrived in Canada and Juile said I was born in May 2007, so God had a plan. His plan was perfect, today fifteen (15) years later, I give God thanks for my three girls, even though they didn't come from my womb and I suffered many disappointments, shame, and ridicule

BROKEN TO BE RESTORED

SERIES 1

I do see the blessings of the Lord in and through my daughters. Because of my daughters, I was able to go back to school and earn two degrees while taking care of them. I would go to school one day per week from 6pm-10pm. I would pick them up from school, give them dinner, shower and help them with their homework and still make it to school. I would get back home by 11pm and be up by 6am to get them ready for school. I finished mt first degree and earned a master's degree in clinical counselling. Today I work as a registered psychotherapist. My daughters have all finished high school. My oldest is 22 years old in November and she works as a PSW and plans to continue nursing. My middle child Nicole, is 20 years old in August and she is going to Carleton University in Ottawa and is doing a major in English and my last child Julie, is 18 years old and just got accepted to Wilfred Laurier University and will be majoring in health sciences.

I Have Decided To Follow Jesus Christ And There Is No Turning Back

Despite the fact that we have come this far by faith, we are still being tested and tried but I have concluded that Satan has already been defeated, and Jesus cannot be defeated, so I will continue to trust in Jesus and let the chips fall where they want. My story has already been told. I am more than a conqueror through Jesus Christ my Lord.

BROKEN TO BE RESTORED

SERIES 1

There is no other place for me and my children but up or the top.

During the pandemic, August 2020 to be exact, I just finished my master's degree and just got a full time job when everywhere was shut down I was the only one with a full time job in an organization that opened its door to help other therapists to get their license, That same year, while I am signing my acceptance letter for my job, I also got the news that my kidneys fail and I had to be on dialysis as soon as picked myself up trusting in the only name I know, Jesus the Christ and continued to push. I bought a cottage at the height of the pandemic to supplement my income.

By January 2023, I lost my primary home and my cottage. I am currently renting a house with my two daughters. Last August 202,4 I started investing money to open my private practice. I spent over 5k, and I did not use my new office one day I was in a coma for 8 days and hospitalized for 44 days. Today I am still learning to walk and must be on modified duties. My baby has been driving around since August 2024 to today. My girls came to the hospital every day and gave me my shower, cooked, cleaned and took care of me and the home while I was in the hospital. I no longer question God and his ways. I choose to be still and wait upon the Lord. His ways are perfect, and I choose to suffer with him so that I can reign with him.

BROKEN TO BE RESTORED

SERIES 1

Letter To My Sister/ Reader

Dear Sister

In the beginning of my letter, it may seem a bit uncertain as to where I was going or what I am saying. For sure we will never get a manual of what will happen each day in our Christian Walk. The bible says that the Just will live by their faith and that's the truth. My faith is not yours nor are your faith mines. We go through our own trials and tribulations every day and we see Christ and glean from what he is trying to teach us. You can't measure the trials or tests on what I went through, you must go through yours and be willing to learn from it. Do not complain, gossip or slander it will just last longer. Stop whining, it will only keep you there longer. The day you learn to praise God through your trials you will get through them faster. You will never go to the next level in ministry or life if you have not overcome the last trial. Trust God, he knows what you need to get you to the next level, not your Pastor or friend. The furnace is as hot as you make it....trust Jesus, he will never give you more than you can bear!

God bless!

Min Marcia

BROKEN TO BE RESTORED

SERIES 1

CHAPTER 4
A NARROW ESCAPE

WRITTEN BY: MARY JOSEPH

"I said, "Lord, be merciful to me;
Heal my soul,
for I have sinned against You.
Psalms 41:4 NKJV

I sat on the hospital bed, with my bible in my hand, staring at the pictures of my children, with tears flowing down my face, I wondered, how did I end up here, how

BROKEN TO BE RESTORED

SERIES 1

did my life become so complicated? I knew that my mother must have been praying, warring, and bombarding hell on my behalf. Voices of condemnation swirled in my head. I felt ashamed, angry, hurt, and frustrated. Sleep evaded my eyes and thoughts of suicide took over my mind. I was angry at myself; I felt lost frustrated and broken.
How could I walk away from God? I could feel the hand of God moving heavily upon me. I was in desperation and wanted nothing else but to surrender to God. I would love to tell you that I did surrender to God but unfortunately, I did not, I continued to listen to the lies of the enemy as accusations after accusation howled at me, Accusations of rape, abortions, and molestation. I was convinced that God was disappointed in me, and I was just as disappointed in him. I prayed over and over in my mind asking God to help me escape this horrible nightmare. Before I could finish my prayer, the nurse interrupted my thoughts "it's time for you to see the doctors." She announced. The stories shared with me about my survival led me to believe that a spirit of death was looming over my family. I was the fourth girl, born to my parents, but the first to live. Four of my sisters died, three of them before I was born and one after my birth. They suffered the same fate. I was told by my mom that my dad's dream was to have a little girl but each time a girl was born they died at the age of six months.

BROKEN TO BE RESTORED

SERIES 1

I can't begin to understand what my parents went through. Even thinking of this now seemed mystical. So I asked myself!

Why did I live and my sisters died? Mom told me that my godmother took me to a Hindu temple where a pundit performed Hindu rituals to save my life. He then placed a mark on my forehead with ashes. This was a common practice in Trinidad for the parents mainly mothers to take their children to the Hindu temple seeking help from the priest to remove marasmus. I am indignant about the claim that the Hindu priest saved my life. I know for sure that God will preserve my life Jehovah Rap ha deliver me from death, no one or no other God will get the glory. My parents lived in Trinidad before I was born. After my birth, my dad was deported back to St. Vincent, so obviously my mother followed him. As you can tell I was born on the twin island of Trinidad and Tobago, but was raised on the island of St. Vincent & the Grenadines.

Our life was very simple. My dad worked while my mom took care of us. In my early years my parents were not married and neither of them served the lord. Even though mom was not a born again Christian at that stage, she committed herself to taking us to church on Sundays and different services in the week. She made certain we were involved in the church activities. My mom loved the lord but living a common-law life prevented her from committing to God.

BROKEN TO BE RESTORED

SERIES 1

This didn't detour her from doing her daily practices. She prayed a lot, always singing or whistling. My mother memorized most of the Psalms and so she will use these Psalms to pray whenever she is faced with a difficult situation. Finally, at the age of 6 my parents got married and my mom got baptized. My mother became a spiritual leader in our home. Mom relies on the holy spirit to guide her. Many times we were spared from danger because Mom had a dream or a vision. On several occasions she was able to hear an audible voice warning her of impending danger. I have come to know that voice as the voice of the Holy Spirit. Jesus spoke of the Holy Spirit in the book of John. 26 But the Comforter (Counselor, Helper, Intercessor, Advocate, Strengthener, Standby), the Holy Spirit, Whom the Father will send in My name [in My place, to represent Me and act on My behalf], He will teach you all things. And He will cause you to recall (will remind you of, bring to your remembrance) everything I have told you. John 14:26. I listened to mom as she repeated scripture over and over, so I was able to memorize scripture from hearing it.

Not long after my dad who was the financial provider lost his job. He met in a vehicular accident. He lost the use of his left hand. My dad turned to alcohol. Even as a child I knew that my dad was trying to numb the pain in his hand and deal with the fact that he was not able to provide for his family.

BROKEN TO BE RESTORED

SERIES 1

I remembered on that faithful Sunday afternoon, at the age of nine, when our lives were turned upside down. I was sitting in the back of the house, after lunch when we received the news that Dad was in a vehicular accident and they feared he was dead. I remember running to the bathroom in the back, as I knelt down crying I prayed a simple prayer "Please God don't take my daddy." From there on life became difficult for us. Dad started drinking a lot. He became an alcoholic. This caused a lot of turmoil in our home, my siblings and I witnessed and suffered much emotional, physical, and mental abuse. My parents were a prime example of the scripture in Amos 3:3 that states, "Can two walk together, unless they are agreed?" Looking back I feel like church was a place we all found peace. I got baptized at the tender age of eight we spent a lot of time in church. Mom was involved in planning concerts and of course my sibling and I were given a part in the play too. Most of the play was from the bible.
She was quite the stage director and manager. Concerts were planned around the months of April, August, and December. We would make frequent visits to the church. For rehearsals. Rehearsals were also scheduled at home where my siblings and I practiced poems, plays, and songs. Even though things were difficult at home, I will say I was very sheltered, protected by my dad, and guarded by my brothers, while under the watchful eye of my mother. One would think that with all these safeguards, I was well protected. No one was allowed to

BROKEN TO BE RESTORED

SERIES 1

She was quite the stage director and manager. Concerts were planned around the months of April, August, and December. We would make frequent visits to the church. For rehearsals. Rehearsals were also scheduled at home where my siblings and I practiced poems, plays, and songs. Even though things were difficult at home, I will say I was very sheltered, protected by my dad, and guarded by my brothers, while under the watchful eye of my mother. One would think that with all these safeguards, I was well protected. No one was allowed to
break through those safety protocols. Unfortunately they didn't. They lived within the safety of our community which was an extension of my family. They were trusted individuals with easy access to me, that knew how and when to strike.
Growing up I was a quiet child and even though I knew my family would do anything to protect me from anyone and anything I kept quiet about the abuse I had suffered at the hands of relatives. I was scared and talking about sex was a taboo among us. I felt if I had shared what I was experiencing with my family. I believe someone would be hurt my first recollection of this abuse happened at the age of four or five. I hated confrontations that could potentially lead to quarrels, fights, and violence. I hated being the centre of attention especially a negative one. As I grew older I began to speak out. I remember one incident at the age of twelve while visiting a relative.

BROKEN TO BE RESTORED

SERIES 1

I allotted my cousin of an incident that occurred during the night. I was awakened by a relative, an older teenager John, who tried to force himself on me. Fearing that it would happen again I told my cousin. She began to look out for me. The next night she pretended to be asleep she caught him in the act as she tried to cross over her to get to me. The situation was neutralized, and she exposed John to my family. I can't tell you how shameful this was for me. After that incident, a young man who was a friend John stopped me to relay his disappointment and disgust in what John did to me. I was embarrassed when I realized that other people besides my family knew about the incident. This was never spoken of up until today. Yet I carried the shame for a long time.

There was another situation where one of my father's acquaintances tried to lure me away from home. I went to my dad and told him about the conversation Mr B had with me. Dad flew into a rage and went looking for him carrying a concealed machete with him. I was relieved that Dad never found him. Dad send message upon message hoping he would come talk to him, and so he avoided our village. We never saw him again. All of these experiences taught me one thing that I was targeted. I became an expert at recognizing when someone was paying me too much attention. I became self conscious I was careful about the way I dress, stand and sit. I avoided certain places and areas.

BROKEN TO BE RESTORED

SERIES 1

This was my way of avoiding any attempts of sexual misconduct against me. After a while things become very difficult at home. My parents struggled to feed us. Dad found a job to work as a foreman to supervise people as they clean the street. I dreaded Paydays, as soon as dad received his salary he headed for the shop where he brought alcohol and drank until he was drunk. He would staggered home without any money in his pocket.

One day my half-brother visited us from Trinidad and he asked if I would like to visit Trinidad, seeing that I was born there. With my parent's approval I said yes. Looking at the situation at home Mom decided to travel to Trinidad with me. In hope that she would find a job to help the situation at home.

Mom and I moved to Trinidad, but I was very unhappy at first because I missed my siblings. Although I was relieved to be free from all the responsibilities and daily chores, I missed my family. I was the eldest girl and that came with lots of responsibility. My visit to Trinidad was supposed to be a short visit, but I decided I wanted to stay. I did everything in my power to make it happen. I applied for a technical school and I was admitted there to start my nursing career. My training led me into a permanent position. I was excited because now I can shop for my younger sibling and take care of my family financially.

BROKEN TO BE RESTORED

SERIES 1

We found a church and we became members of the church. I loved the lord and so I continue to serve the lord faithfully. Now that I had a Job things seemed much easier. At age eighteen, Stan a Seventh-day Adventist boy came to my mother asking for him to date me. Although he began talking about marriage we only dated for a few months, then it was over before I knew it.

I was bold so I would share the good news of the gospel in school, on buses and on the street. Things started changing because I took my eyes off of God, and I placed them on my mentor. Dolly, not her name. I admired Dolly and I thought she was a God fearing woman. I realized now that I held her in high esteem, as if she could do no wrong. That's where I was wrong. The bible warns us in Exodus 34:14 For you shall worship no other god; for the Lord, whose name is Jealous, is a jealous (impassioned) God. Once I learned of my mentor's infidelity. I was so disappointed that I lost my zeal for God. This started my journey of running away from God. My mom returned home without me and my dad wasn't happy. I began to hang out with the wrong people. One day I met this young man I thought he really liked me. I was invited to his house to meet his family; after meeting his family he took me downstairs to hang out. Before I knew it the cousin disappeared. He began to kiss me; I tried to stop him when I noticed he wanted to go beyond the kiss.

BROKEN TO BE RESTORED

SERIES 1

He held me down and raped me. After he took me home, I knew I never wanted to see him again.
I wondered how many girls he did this to. I was disappointed angry and nervous.
I began to ponder "what if I'm pregnant?" I thought. Just about this time I met up with a young man whom I used to talk to, but had lost contact with. We began to go out again. After a few weeks I realized I had missed my period. I began to panic. How do I tell my present boyfriend I was pregnant? So I avoided him. Here I am pregnant; I lost my job, about to get kicked out of my place. How did my life become so complicated? I sank into depression. To make matters worse my mother returned to Trinidad. Even though I was happy to see her I really didn't want to be around her at this point in my life. I knew she would be disappointed in me. I moved in with her, and she began to question me about my pregnancy. I denied it. I went to one of my friends for advice; and of course, she painted my situation to be one of hopelessness. She convinced me that Abortion was the only way out. She said the baby at this stage has not been developed, and that it was easy to abort. I was desperate I believed her. On the abortion table I was scared and so I thought of stopping the abortion, but before I knew it. The lady announced that it was over. I felt nothing at first but after a few hours I began to have unbearable pain. I carried my dead baby for six days before I actually went into labour. I could have died. My life was in absolute chaos.

BROKEN TO BE RESTORED

SERIES 1

My heart is so broken, I just can't stop crying. I knew I had to gain some perspective in my life, so I began to job hunt. I went to an interview I returned home, feeling tired and drained from the hot sun. I fell asleep only to be awakened by the landlord's hand caressing me. When I retaliated, he pulled out a knife that looked like a small dagger it was long and thin. He demanded sex and told me he would kill me and drink
poison after. He then showed me the bottle with poison and he gave me a letter to read that he had written to his daughter who was my age. I was overcome with fear, but I tried to remain calm. I came up with a plan and told him I would do nothing without protection, he explained that he's been watching me for a long time, and he wanted me so badly, I told him that I didn't want to get pregnant again and I asked if he had any pills. He turned away, with the knife in his hand and I jumped over the bed head and ran for the door leading to another bedroom. The door was locked, but I was able to unlock it before he got to me. I ran to the back door, but it was locked. I sat on the floor and kicked until the door flew open. I jumped down into an area that was under construction and landed between some steel rods that was being used to make a pillar. I had a narrow escape by avoiding those steel rods, that by itself was a miracle.

I believe the angel of protected me. He threw the knife at me with such power the knife got stuck in the door as it violently waved back and forth.

BROKEN TO BE RESTORED

SERIES 1

I got up and ran to the neighbour's. She was expecting me she said she wasn't sure when he would strike. I was told that she was wondering if we really knew him, because he was arrested once before for the murder of a young lady. She also explained, that he walked her home from a party, and the next morning she was found dead in the ditch. I waited at the neighbour's home until my brother and mom got home. He was confronted but he denied everything, claiming I was the one that came on to him. I can see that my brother wanted to strangle him, and would have done it if Mom wasn't there. My brother accompanied us to the house to pack our things. We left immediately

After a couple of years Mom travelled back home, and I was on my own again. One night I went to a crusade, and I met Ray he began to pursue me. I ignored him. I knew he was in a relationship and so I wanted nothing to do with him. He assured me that he was single. I was very cautious around him because of my experience in the past. I was afraid to go out with him, so whenever he invited me out, I would never show up. I was hoping he would give up and leave me alone. One day he was invited to join him at his brother's wedding reception.

I excepted. He introduced me to his parents. His mom took an instant liking to me. At this time I was living with my brother and his girlfriend. They began to have some problems so they split up and I was left alone in the apartment. The landlord had promised the apartment to someone else, so I was asked to moved out and moved in with a girlfriend close to Al's house.

BROKEN TO BE RESTORED

SERIES 1

After a couple of he months living with my friend her boyfriend came home early from work one day and tried to rape me. I thought "here we go again". I had just arrived home and was about to change but I was determined that I am not going down without a fight. I found the strength to fight him off. I told Ray about the incident and he insisted that I moved in with him.. Even though I met him when I first moved to Trinidad, I felt like I didn't know him, and I had commitment issues. Ray threatened to tell my friend about the incident. I didn't want things to get weird between us, so I agreed to move in with him. My girlfriend was not happy that I moved out.

I just told her that I felt like a burden. I thought this is temporary, but before I knew it, one year had passed and I was pregnant with our first daughter shortly after our second daughter was born. Al's job took him away from home to another island, sometimes he would be gone for months. Things began to change between us. Al was always home late smelling of alcohol. I ignored and pretended things weren't falling apart. Then I found out he had impregnated another woman. Our relationship got worse after I met Al and the woman out on a date.

I decided to leave and visit a close relative Hans. After one week I returned home, but Al said I wasn't welcome there. I was relieved but I wanted my children to leave with me. I wondered to myself where I am going to live. The thought of homelessness with my babies was overwhelming.

BROKEN TO BE RESTORED

SERIES 1

Al began to use our children as a pawn. He refused to let me see them.

I was forced to return to Hans. After a couple of weeks Al asked if I could come and watch the kids. I was excited just to spend some time with them, even if it was on his terms. Sometimes he pretended to be working so I could come over. One night Hans said he needed to talk to me. He invited me to go house hunting with a cousin. On our way home after dropping off our cousin, he decided to stop at a park.

We began to talk about the problem I was having with Al. I was so relieved to finally talk to someone. Instead of talking about Al, he began to reminisce about the first time he met me. Talked about the fact that I was sixteen and a virgin. I was so naive that I didn't pick up on the cues that tell me he was up to no good. He got out of the car and moved around and opened my side of the door. He took me by surprise and pushed the seat backwards, before I knew it his mouth was over mine. I moved my head trying to resist his kiss. I fought with him, he pinned me down, and I continued to fight. I could feel the sweat dripping onto my forehead. When he was done I broke out in tears his words to me were 'look what we've done" then he swore that we were not related because his parent is not my relative. I wanted to run away, but I was frozen in disbelief.

BROKEN TO BE RESTORED

SERIES 1

How could this be happening to me again?
We drove back to the house in silence.
The next day I packed and left. I told our cousin what he did. I became depressed.

At this time Al began to show up at my job blocking anyone he thought was interested in me. He asked me to move back home, and I refused I was very unhappy and depressed. Al promised to move out if I move in, I agree. Al would visit us often, even though he was living with another woman. I was tired of his games. He kept moving in and out. I was so depressed that I hardly slept.
I prayed each day asking God for sleep to come to my eyes. I began to have suicidal thoughts, but I knew if I took my life I would go to hell. I went to drug store and began to look for antidepressant, but they were of no help to meI was at my lowest, when I received a message that one of my half brothers was in a boat accident and died, and they couldn't find his body. I went to the nurse's quarters and cried for hours. The head nurse took me to her office, and she tried to help, but I refused to talk. Finally she gave me instructions to go and see a counsellor at the mental institution. My girlfriend took my children home with her and I was told that they cried all night. After speaking to the counsellor, she referred me to a doctor.
My session with the doctor was very intense.
He was surprised that I was still in my right mind.

BROKEN TO BE RESTORED

SERIES 1

He advised me to spend the night at the safe house. These were houses set up away from the hospital that people who need rest would go to. I agree and I was given a yellow pill that knocks me out.

The next morning I was awoken by a nurse. Remembering my children, I told the nurse that I needed to leave, so I could go home to prepare my children for school. The nurse looked at me with sadness and advised me. "I am sorry but you must first see the doctors, so they can release you." I sat back down on the edge of the bed, thinking about how my children will get to school I stared at the picture of my children. l began to pray in my mind asking God to help me escape this horrible nightmare. Before I could finish my prayer, the nurse interrupted my thoughts "It's time for you to see the doctors." She announced. I was guided to a room with a panel of doctors sitting at a large table. I scanned the room searching for a familiar face like the face of the doctor who admitted me the night before, he made me feel comfortable as if he understood what I was going through. Maybe he was an angel. I knew they were going to question me and I would have to rehash the traumatic events that led up to my admittance to the hospital. I felt like I was being interrogated by the doctor. I spoke about the rape that led up to the abortion.

The doctor prescribed some sleeping pills to help me sleep, these were only to be taken at the hospital.

BROKEN TO BE RESTORED

SERIES 1

My request to return to my home was denied, instead they requested that I spend a few nights so they can monitor me. They cautioned me to move away from home for about a week, and encouraged me to rest, bath in the sea and eat lots of fish. I knew that I wasn't an ordinary case. My case was not a psychological case. My case was a prodigal daughter running away from her father. After I left the hospital I knew I had to get away; so I packed up my daughters and sent them to my parents in St. Vincent with the intention to join them soon after.Al was furious with me for sending away his children. He sent messages to me threatening me. I began to move from place to place.

Al's dad offered me a room downstairs, to stay while I prepare to join my children. Al lived with his girlfriend, so I wondered what his reason was for his constant visits to his parents home. I tried my best to avoid him, but it wasn't long after he decided to move into the same room with me. I kept my distance. It was awkward having him there, since we were not intimate. things between us got intense. We were in constant fights. I began to attend church, and prayed fervently. I begged and cried, and I made promises to God. I prayed, "Lord please relieve me of this relationship". My answer came one Thursday in February at 2. p.m. I suddenly had a thought, it was as if a voice was talking to me. "If you don't leave this man, he will kill you with a gun or by Aids". I was horrified. I immediately got up travelled to Port of Spain and purchased a ticket to St. Vincent.

BROKEN TO BE RESTORED

SERIES 1

My mother explained what happened on that Thursday in February, at 2 pm. She said that on that day a group of people came to see her. They were in a prayer and fasting service when the leader Mrs L had a vision of me being drifted from my parent's home. She travelled to the countryside to talk to my mom. They began to pray, and Mrs L called out my name, commanding me to come home. On that same Thursday I bought a ticket to St. Vincent I told Al family that I was leaving for St. Vincent. Some of them joked saying I will be back, Al tried to be nice to me asking me to bring our children home. I assure him that I will bring them back.

To convince him I showed him my returned ticket that was good for 6 months. I told him that I wanted to spend a couple of months with my parents, then I will return with the children. I didn't want to travel by plane so I travelled to St. Vincent on a passenger ferry boat that cruised around the Caribbean islands. Al followed me to the port and he begged me to promise that I would return with the children I actually felt sorry for him knowing that I was never coming back.

I boarded the ferry and found a comfortable seat on deck, so I could look at Trinidad as it disappeared in the distance. As the ship sailed by I realized I was able to see my home. I waved goodbye whispering to myself saying "Goodbye, Trinidad I don't know if I will ever see you again" I did see Trinidad but I never did see Al. Tears burn my cheek as it flow down my face.

BROKEN TO BE RESTORED

SERIES 1

As the night passed I couldn't sleep. I was excited to see my children. At 5am I decided to walk out onto the deck. I could see the Island coming into view. I breathe a sigh of relief and muttered under my breath "I am home. Immediately it felt as if someone had removed the heavy load I didn't know I was carrying. I arrived in St. Vincent excited to see my girls this was the first time in a year I felt so light as if I had dropped 100 pounds.
I arrived at my parents home and the dog welcomed me. Mom said he always barks when anyone comes to the house. My dad hugged me and cried. I had never seen my dad cr,y his long lost daughter was finally home. I couldn't wait for school to be over, so I went to the school that is across the street. The principal who used to be my teacher was there I found a job and began to support my children. Al called, asking when we were coming home. I told him I am home and this has become my children home. Life was much better for us. One day I received a call from one of his sister- In-laws, she advised me to move to Canada with my sister. Al wanted to join us in St. Vincent. I was heartbroken; I knew it wasn't about the children it was about me I had to leave my children again.I flew out and came to Canada. I then applied to the Canadian Government.
At this point I made a conscious decision to rededicate my life to God. I had an interview with Immigration Canada, and the officer advised me to get proof in the form of a letter from the Police or Hospital, describing the account of my suffering.

BROKEN TO BE RESTORED

SERIES 1

After many attempts, I was amazed that the very thing that brought shame in my life, God used it to free me. Genesis 50:20 "But as for you, you meant evil against me; but God meant it for good, in order to bring it about as it is this day, to save many people alive." I was able to obtain a letter from the mental hospital. What the enemy meant for bad God turned it around for good.

After five years I was able to be reunited with my children. In order for us to be landed in this country, Al had to sign the children over to me. He promised to sign, but he just ignored me. I went on a series of fasting asking God to speak to his heart. A couple of days after I broke the fast I received a message saying that Al died three weeks ago. He died of HIV complications (AIDS). We were heartbroken; I could feel my children's pain. What do I say to them? They never got to say goodbye. I was very surprised when they told me they were sad he was dead but happy I got away. Glory be to God.

BROKEN TO BE RESTORED

SERIES 1

A LETTER TO MY SISTER/READER

To you who suffered in silence

I declare to you today that God is breaking your silence and you're not alone. God loves you no matter what you've done; there is nothing you can do to make God change his mind about you. His love is unconditional and is everlasting. Listen as he speaks to you from his words" saying: "Yes, I have loved you with an everlasting love; Therefore with loving kindness I have drawn you. Jeremiah 31:3b. Come on girl! Don't you know he sees your pain and he knows what you're going through? His arm is wide open, waiting for you. There are unlimited resources for you. His words state "And my God shall supply all your need according to His riches in glory by Christ Jesus."Philippians 4:13,
God wants to bring you to a place of peace. He's got your back, and don't worry, we're here with you. No more loneliness. This road might be rough, but you can call on him at anytime. You can do all things through Christ who strengthens you Phil 4:19..
I know this can be difficult, but releasing forgiveness is important for your healing, so I forgive those who has hurt me and spitefully. Use me He will turn your scars into stars. This is not the end. This is your beginning.

A Prayer

Heavenly Father, I come to you in the name of Jesus Christ of Nazareth. I ask for forgiveness for all my sins. Lord would you please heal my broken heart .
Thank you for your protection.
Thank you for preserving my life.
Lord, I know. If it had not been for the Lord who was on my side. When men rose up against me then they would have [quickly] swallowed me alive, when their wrath was kindled against me." Today I choose to cast all my cares on you. I cast all seed of bitterness unforgiveness, worries, pain, anger, rage, and wrath.
I declare Psalms 124:7 AMP "I have escaped like a bird from the snare of the fowlers; The trap is broken and we have escaped."
God, I receive all the good things you have in store for me. For it is written in the book of Jeremiah 29:11, "For I know the plans and thoughts that I have for you,' says the Lord, 'plans for peace and well-being and not for disaster, to give you a future and a hope."
Despitefully Amen

BROKEN TO BE RESTORED

SERIES 1

CHAPTER 5
BROKEN FOR GOD'S TIMING

WRITTEN BY: LORRAINE DAWSON

"He has made everything beautiful in its time. He has also set eternity in the human heart; yet no one can fathom what God has done from beginning to end."
Ecclesiastes 3:11 NIV

BROKEN TO BE RESTORED

SERIES 1

Dear future me;

Hey beautiful Women of God,
You've been bent but not broken
You over came being a single mother
You started a business in the midst of your storm
You had a fail marriage BUT
You got married to the one sent you, the man of your dreams

You became a homeowner
Your children are all grown, successful and thriving
Every word God has spoken over your life has come to pass.
Mighty Women of God !

Before you got here let me tell you a little about how you got here and where it all began. I met him when I was about 14 turning 15. It was a summer of august and my mom took my brother and myself to Jamaica for a family vacation and just like any other child I was excited, but I never knew that would be the beginning of ups and downs, nightmares and pain. Because it opened more doors to some of the sexual things I had to under go through in my teenage years

So one day I was staying at my cousin's house and you know in Jamaica. The vibes is always right so I was in the

BROKEN TO BE RESTORED

SERIES 1

front yard and I was dancing with my little cousin who I'm very close to and this gentleman who was a friend of or the best friend I should say of my cousin was there, and to my surprising he took set on me.

So you know I was doing a little thing dancing whining my little tiny waist and just having fun he came over. He introduced himself and we got through talking now. At this time. I believe I was about 14 years old going on 15 cause I just had started high school And you know me never really being in love I met this handsome wonderful Jamaican tall brown skin man, and I fell madly in love with him.
So there was a car in the driveway and we went into the car and we started to talk and I don't really remember what the conversation was about but all I remember is then him kissing me and loving upon me. Later that night you know we would hang out in Jamaica. They're not really strict on age when people are going to party and I had older cousins that I would hang out with so I blended in anyways I remember going to the party and he's showing up and I had my foot I think my foot on another person's lap, which is a male because my foot was tired and he was a friend of the family and he shows up and he was like upset because you know, I guess he already claimed me as his woman or his girl Anyway later that night we stayed out on the veranda or in Canadian terms the porch and we would talk and make out and stay outside till wee hours of the morning, but I didn't just stop there one night. I went to his house and I never really shared this with anybody.

BROKEN TO BE RESTORED

SERIES 1

I went in his room. I lay on his bed. The music was playing. The mood was set and he came over to me we were kissing you was touching. You know, doing all that stuff until he went lower and went into my underpants where he penetrated my lady parts with his fingers, and it felt so good , Did I stop him? Did I like it? I have to be honest yes because that was pretty much my first time and I fell in love with him, so I was willing to do anything that he wanted me to do.
When I look back on his actions I realized that it wasn't right what he did because I was under aged and he was much older than me I guess in a way I was molested and taken advantage of , I thank God that I never went further where he used his man part to also penetrate my Lady part. How many of us have been there where we let someone who we trusted and loved explore our bodies this way.

Fast forward, Jamaica and became a long distance couple it went on and on for a few years you know even my mom's Rogers phone bill like $2000 just talking with him and staying on the phone with him night and day after a while we lost touch. I really can't even explain to your tell you really what happened but we lost each other's contact and I moved on with my life and I met my first baby father which I have two kids for him and so on, but that's another story for another time moving along years went by and because I always was in love with this man. He was always a person that I wanted to be with.

BROKEN TO BE RESTORED

SERIES 1

There was no question. There was no if there was no, but he is the one that I wanted when I was always going through problems, he would be the one that I would talk to and call and he would make me laugh and he talking down and stuff like
It was December 2016 when we reconnected and I was going back out to Jamaica for a wedding in January so I invited him to my family's house. We spent two weeks together and for the two weeks was up.
We decided that we were going to get married and at that time that was the time that we actually Became physically sexually active for the first time.
During this time I made a trip out to Jamaica by myself cause by this time I've already had four kids, so I went back to Jamaica to spend a couple weeks with him just so that we can you know be alone and date each other and I tell you could you not this is one of the best times of my life because you know I get to be with the man that I always dreamt about always wanted to be my husband and we were going to get married and at this time I met his mother and his family and his children because he also had kids on the outside just like I did and we were OK with that. We came to mutual agreement that we both made mistakes but now we want to settle down and make it right and go forward and that's just what we did.

So now I started to plan my wedding and it was slowly approaching, which was August 18, 2018 and if you look

BROKEN TO BE RESTORED

SERIES 1

closely on the date August which is the eighth month stands for new beginnings and I really thought that I was getting a new beginning I was head over heels in love. I was excited I was happy. I packed up all my family my mom and my sister and my kids some aunts and we went to Jamaica for a week got married and in that time of being in Jamaica just for one week I came back and I found out that I was pregnant with my last Babygirl that I have now the good thing about it was she was conceived in marriage so I was on the right track because I had went back into church with my two foot in.

Little did I know that my fairytale, happy ending was about to unravel, I had the baby and she was just a few months when I took her to first meet her dad in Jamaica. We went to his mom's house this day because her house. Would be more comfortable and suitable for the baby and my other children as well as myself in less than 24 hours I don't know what happened. I don't know when things spiral but all I remember was him cursing me out and me picking up the phone, calling my cousin in Kingston to come and get me This is where the emotional abuse started. He called me all sorts of names and told me I was this, and I was that he belittled me.
He put me down. He made me feel like I was nothing at that point. I didn't even feel like I was his wife, the mother of his child who just gave birth a few months ago, so what did I do? I packed up and I left he left the house and while he left, I packed up my kids and all of our belongings and

BROKEN TO BE RESTORED

SERIES 1

I left but guess what that was short-lived
 because I was so in love with him and I was willing to fight for a marriage. I stayed and I worked things out with him. A few years went by and by this time now we're in the lockdown and I have to say that 2020 was one of the best years out of my four year marriage was the best year I've ever had in my marriage. I don't know if it was because we all thought we were gonna die and you know we were just trying to make the best of life, but I'm grateful and I thank God for That experience and all the experiences that I had in that marriage.
I remember when I used to get a lot of dreams dreams that I would see my husband cheating on me with people that I knew and when I would tell him about them, he would say you're crazy a foolishness that will never happen right I believe them because this was the man that I loved The man that I said I do too and boy to my surprise was I shocked when everything that was in the dark came to light, but let's rewind a little bit in this relationship this marriage I was unhappy I never even got the beer minimum everything he did for me when he did it was because he was pretty much forced to. He never treated me like his queen he never treated me like he loved me yes he may have said the things, but there was no actions behind his words.

BROKEN TO BE RESTORED

SERIES 1

He made me feel like I was nothing and undeserving of love but because I still forgot and I took vowels and I'm in a covenant, I honoured it because he was my husband the hurts and the pain, the abuse, especially when we would have fights things that you would say hurt me to the core made me look at myself differently. Maybe I'm not pretty enough. Maybe I'm not thick enough. Maybe I'm not worthy enough to be loved unconditionally. I was always that woman who never asked a man for anything until this day, I still haven't given up hope that one day all these things that I so desire will be mine. No, I haven't given up. Hope I believe that God will grant me all the desires of my heart And more but this girl, this woman that you see was broken. I know I'm not fully healed from all the past trauma and the words that he spoke over my life, but it's a working progress. I am broken for God's timing and we all know that God's timing is the best timing so back to the abuse he's never physically put his hands on me but mentally spiritually and emotionally I felt like I was dead.

I was doing so well in church finish Bible school and was about to be appointed and because of the things that my husband was putting me through and the things that he was doing, I was stripped a strip of a lot of things I was doing things that I wasn't supposed to do I was going places that I wasn't supposed to go, but God and I emphasize this, but GOD. If it wasn't for his grace and mercy and the calling on my life I don't know where I would be.

BROKEN TO BE RESTORED

SERIES 1

Some more time had passed and now we are going into our fourth year of marriage so I decided that I would go to Jamaica and spend for the first time of our fourth anniversary together. I was excited because this would've been the first time we were celebrated together in person. During my stay, my ex husband would.

Leave me at the house hours at a time and I never questioned it because I was never really a person that like to be on the road so I would let him do his thing because you know as a wife your husband goes out you know that he's coming back home to you One day we're there and I could never seem to remember why these arguments would start to happen but we got into it, and it was really big. It was never physical, but his words the words that he said it was like they had a power because they pierced through my heart like a sphere and I would say to myself how could this man Tell me that I am ungrateful and tell me all these words and say all these mean things that hurt me when I left my children to come and spend a month with him I spend my money, my hard-working money to make sure we have everything that we needed because he never had a job he never worked And he could not maintain me.

I was the financial breadwinner in the marriage and I got to a point where I even have to call my aunt to come and get me even though it was late at night and she said Lorraine I can't get a ride to come and get you now

BROKEN TO BE RESTORED

SERIES 1

but sleep and if you feel the same way you feel in the morning I will come so morning came and of course I changed my mind because we woke up and we weren't seeing much to each other, but I
said I'm gonna stay and give I'll try because it was almost time for me to go home anyways I think I had about a week left and we enjoy this week But there was something off about this time because when we would have sexual intercourse, it was different I couldn't really put my finger on it as to why I thought it was just because he was stressed.
I was stressed and you know we had a little disagreement only to come back to Canada and one month later my ex-husband would have stop talking to me completely. I don't know what I did. I don't know what I said. I went over this in my mind over and over and over I went through our chats to see what did I say anything this man cut me and our daughter Completely off no warning nothing for months I didn't hear from him October November December I would cry I would cry from their pain I felt I beat myself up. I blamed myself. I cursed myself thinking that I was the one that was the problem, but listen to this.

It was January 2023 and I was going on a Daniel fast and I remember asking God on the first day of the fast gone let your perfect and divine will for my marriage manifest. I said God if this marriage is not to be God, I promise you I won't get mad if you want us to separate to be a part to divorce I will not be mad. Guess what? What couple weeks later before the fast end in my best friend came to me and she

BROKEN TO BE RESTORED

SERIES

said Bestie I wanna tell you something but I don't know how to tell you and I said tell me she said Bestie I don't know how to tell you you're gonna hate me no mama let's go outside and talk. I'm sure by this now you can figure out what I'm about to say my best friend said your husband called me said yeah and the things that he said about you best friend so low was so degrading. He was putting all the blame on you and seeing you this and your son also sort of things, but I didn't finish talking to him on the phone and that was it was about to be January 15, which is his birthday and she said the Holy Spirit told her to call him this was about 11:59 Pm and when she called a woman answer the phone now this woman wasn't me because i'm here in Canada and he's in Jamaica.

He was cheating on me that this has been going on for quite some time, but it never was revealed until this very moment this woman who answer the phone cussed out my best friend and cussed out him came on the phone. She was giving it to him telling him her mind. I said oh I just wanted some vagina and all these things, but it wasn't that it was just a one-time thing. I'll never see you again. He had a relationship with this other woman he left me and his family for another woman and till up to a few months ago, as I write this, he was with this woman, but now this woman has ended things with him because I'm sure she's figured out he ain't worth anything. Anything ain't anything but extra baggage and the funny thing is they don't even know the curse that they just

BROKEN TO BE RESTORED

SERIES

placed upon themselves, but yeah, it was revealed that my ex-husband was seeing someone else for years in our marriage and I never knew I mean I wasn't naïve about it. I did have the dreams, and I felt like I couldn't trust him and stuff like that but because I loved him and I said oh this is my marriage is my family. I'm going to make it work I stayed and I tried even not getting the bare minimum even through all the mental and emotional abuse. This man put me through. I stayed, but it doesn't end there. I have more to share, however, as I go along, I will open up more to you, but this is just a little piece of my journey where I have been broken for God's timing

What God has started in my life he will continue story be continued…

Letter To My Sister/ Reader

To The Beautiful Women Reading This
Repeat after me ...

I AM beautiful
I AM loved
I AM strong
I AM a conqueror
I AM creative
I AM God masterpiece
I AM blessed
I AM prosperous
I AM healed
I AM favored
I AM peace
I AM joy
I AM who God says I am
I AM ME!!!

These are the words I tell myself now ! But it wasn't always like this, I am not the wound I am the women who survived it ,I have made mistakes but you will never see me quit Turn Your pressure into prayer

Father God I thank you for your grace and your mercy, I thank you that you have brought this wonderful women reading this prayer out of her pit , out of her storm, mighty God I pray that you will heal all the wounds and broken pieces in the mighty name of Jesus . father

I pray that she is being restored and renewed,
Lord your word says that we can do all things through Christ who
gives us strength and so Father God   thanks for all that you're doing
and about to do in her life in Jesus mighty name I pray amen

I Love You, Jesus Loves You!

" God is within her, she can not fall; God will help her at break of day".

BROKEN TO BE RESTORED

SERIES 1

CHAPTER 6
AFTER HER PASSING

WRITTEN BY: CAROL JOHNSON

HER LAST DAY.

Her last day, March 13, will be a day that would forever be etched into the chronicles of my consciousness. Why you may ask? Well, I'll let you in on my story, one that's filled with family trauma, betrayal, greed, unforgiveness, and at this point the whole kitchen sink of human emotions is all lined up to take it's place in my story

BROKEN TO BE RESTORED

SERIES 1

about her passing. My beloved sister My-Anne. I detest that ill-fated day that took you away from me. That ill fated day when you passed from your physical body that was riddled with sores and went on to put on your immortal body to live your blessed eternal life with the ancestors. Yes, you heard it right. She passed away from this God forsaken, corrupted world to live her best life in the great beyond. In the grand scheme of things I think we have this whole birth and death ideology all backwards. To quote scripture, Ecclesiastes 7:1, "A good name is better than fine perfume, and the day of death better than the day of birth." That is to say in so many words, to rejoice when one dies and mourn when one is born. But we, fragile vessels that we are, here one day and gone the next, are giddy with excitement at a new birth and, completely shattered when a loved one passes from this earth.

So, I will give the *"rules"* the proverbial middle finger and continue to do it how it's been done for centuries. I was completely and utterly devastated at the loss of my kindred spirit, my ride or ride, my headstrong, brilliant, financially savvy, Obama loving sister, My-Anne. The disease that had ravaged her once picture perfect skin with sores and lesions in the end had won. She was barely recognizable. Head to toe was discolored and covered with sores that oozed bright pink pus. A foul order emitted from her and I was utterly flabbergasted that this was happening to my sister. I felt her pain and shame as she lay on that hospital bed fighting for her life. The hospital staff, bless their hearts, tried their best to treat her as humane as possible but I could see the pity on their faces.

BROKEN TO BE RESTORED

SERIES 1

I remembered, just a few weeks earlier, about a month or so before her passing, how shocked I had been at the sight of her weak frail thinning body.
You see, as the disease progressed, she had been consulting various doctors to diagnose and treat the condition attacking her skin. But nothing they prescribed or recommended worked. Instead the cancer decided that it was time to ramp up the ante. Her skin started to disintegrate right before our very eyes. I kept looking back at pictures we have taken over the years and saw the progression of the disease in a new light. She had asked me to take her to an appointment with a specialist at one of the top cancer research hospital in the city. When she told me about the appointment I was so full of hope. Hope that it was not too late to treat whatever this sickness was. Hope I could have my sister back to her old self. BRAVE, Smart, bossy, beautiful and full of life.

I had arrived early so we could beat the rush hour traffic going into the city. I did a u turn on her street so I could parked across the house to wait on her. She took some time to ready herself as she tried her best to put herself together. She was in such a weaken state. I texted her to let her know that I was waiting on her across the street. Finally, I saw some movements at the front door and she started to emerge from the house. As she was crossing the street to the car it broke my heart to see that she could barely walk. She looked like a shadow of her former self. I felt my chest tighten like my lungs were refusing to do their job.
 I watched my sister, being the proud and sophisticated person she was, held her head high and tried to walk

BROKEN TO BE RESTORED

SERIES 1

with as much dignity and strength as she could muster. She greeted me with a bright and cheery, good morning and heaved herself down in the front seat. I opened my mouth to say something but swallowed my words. I didn't know what to say.

She was an extremely private person so the rapid decline of her health took us all by surprise. Of course we had noticed that her skin was starting to grossly discolor and was shedding like a snake, peeling away from the tendons on her bones. I shuddered at the thought replaying that particular day over and over and over in my mind. WHAT in name of all that is good and pure in this universe was causing this decay of my sister's body? Whenever we tried to address the elephant in the room she would become really defensive, trying desperately to assure us that she had everything under control.

So, we learnt to tread lightly where her health was concerned. But now, in hindsight, we should have been more proactive instead of reactive with My-Anne and this dreaded sickness. Now, I watched as the skeleton remains of my once beautiful sister took her last breathe on that cold unforgiving hospital bed. The doctors had warned us that she would not make it through the night. She was in such a weakened state the doctor advised that if her heart should stop resuscitation was not an option. But My-Anne, being the bad ass fighter that she was fought on for her life. I held her frail hands and song hymns to her. She squeezed my hands as if to say sing on my sister, sing on.

BROKEN TO BE RESTORED

SERIES 1

Finally, on a somber Tuesday evening, when the world was carrying on with life as usually My-Anne took her last breath, She may have lost the battle but she won the war. She was surrounded by those who loved her dearly and by those who "claimed" to love her. I stood by her bedside for a very long time just looking at her corpse willing her to open her eyes unbelief sticking in my craw like a blub of mucus fighting for it's freedom. The day that we realized that she needed medical intervention and basically forced her to go to the hospital kept repeating in my mind, stuck on replay like the reel in one of those old black and white movie.

I felt like I was in an alternate universe where this sad depressing situation was taking place and, anytime now, any time now, I will be jolted back to the universe where My-Anne and I were the best of friends and, at times, the worst of enemies. I smiled fondly at the memory of our loving but rocky sibling relationship. We loved each other dearly, I being the oldest and she two years younger. She was stubborn and controlling and even though we fought like cats and dogs, our bond was unbreakable.

I could hear the silent sounds of suffering so loud my ears started to protest. We were all standing around her bed, disbelief hanging unto our soul, swallowing the hard truth that she was indeed gone. Our immediate family, our mother and siblings, her nephews and nieces whom she loved and adored, and others who, throughout her life didn't care much for her were in the room.

BROKEN TO BE RESTORED

SERIES 1

And, if we're being totally transparent, she didn't really cared for them either. But, here they stood on her final day on earth, skulking around her bed like vultures.
Oh the hypocrisy!
How do we do it? How do we go on living our lives when one of us, who we remembered was so full of life, has been so viciously taken away? Make you think how woefully unprepared for death we all are.

The Viewing

I arrived at the funeral home feeling like my world was unraveling. These past few days after her passing have been a blur of grief, pain, family infighting, wills, next of kings and funeral arrangements, leaving me drained. My eyes were swollen from crying, my face puffy with sorrow. As family and friends gather to pay their respects, I greeted them with a smile. But my smile was so tight it felt like it might shatter under the weight of my pain. The family had started to unravel. Yes, the years of pent up anger, bitterness and resentment burst forth like the rain in Noah's flood and I and my children have been locked out of the ark. Family members who you thought you knew became strangers. Venom shot from their lips and eyes filled with disdain pierced through the fragile facade of the bond of what was once a family unit.

Across the room, I could see my mother. She had arrived before me and now stood by the casket, holding my little sister close. Their quiet sobs fill the space between them, their grief as fake as the hair on their head. I watched them both, the anger pulsing out of my chest like demons trying to escape hell's fire.

BROKEN TO BE RESTORED

SERIES 1

Are they really sad that My-Anne is gone? I bet a million dollars that you will find no tears, not one god damn drop in their eyes if you should roll up on them by the casket right this minute. Those sounds coming from them are as empty as their hearts.

I found a comfortable chair and sat down wearily into its welcoming folds. I watched as my brother, the fool of fools, walked into the room looking as if he was important. He greeted everyone, feigning sadness as he acknowledged a couple of people then went to stand by the casket with his mom and sister.

Family and friends were starting to arrive in drips and drabs. My-Anne's coworkers arrived in a large group and you could tell she was really loved by them. It's so funny that you never really knew the people your family member worked with until a death or a wedding takes place.

The work family so to speak were mourning My-Anne with more sincerity and sorrow than some of her own blood. Make that make sense! Many brought beautiful floral arrangements and cards which the funeral director gracefully placed at strategic positions around the coffin. It was a beautiful coffin, My-Anne would have approved. It was a total waste of money but her mother was keeping up appearances. "Look at the beautiful coffin that I bought for my daughter" says her attitude as she feigns grief drumming up sympathy.

"Shaking my damn head".

The atmosphere in the funeral parlor with the family was so tense, people could tell that something was off. But, there was no time to play Detective Columbo, we needed to give My-Anne a good send off.

BROKEN TO BE RESTORED

SERIES 1

My-Anne's father is here for the funeral. He is 80 years old but looks as strong as any 70 year old. His wife, who My-Anne will never get the chance to meet is accompanying him to the casket to pay their respect. He stood for a long time just staring at My-Anne, regretting years of estrangement from his daughter, sorrow causing his strong squared jawline to shake quietly. I went to stand with them for support. He whispered softly between tears that this was not how he wanted to see his daughter after 30 years. The fact that years were wasted fighting about who abandoned who seems so unimportant now.

I could see my spoiled entitled little sister walking over to me. I attempted to speak to her husband earlier and he gave me the stink eye. So, what the hell does she want with me now. I'm so frigging over all the drama she and her mother has been slinging at me. They are two peas in a pod I tell you. She is spoiled to the core being the baby of the family. My-Anne knew it and tried to warn me, but I was too stupid to see past her bullshit. She believes that we owe her something.

What, what do we owe you spoiled and rotten child. You always had mom's heart, didn't have to fight for any affection like My-Anne and I had to. You were the golden child and you wanted to hold on to that title cause it what it may. Well it's all yours!

She is saying something to me about some food for the repast. I nodded my head trying to feign an interest. What did she say about the jerk chicken? I really don't give a shit. I'm starting to feel flustered. Maybe it is the hot flashes or my bullshit radar overheating.

BROKEN TO BE RESTORED

SERIES 1

Either way, I excused myself and went to find the bathroom. I need to splash some merciful cold water on my flushed face before I explode. I found an empty stall, went in, locked the doors and just let the tears come. Why hold them back? My friend and confidant is lying in a coffin a few feet away from me. I miss her like crazy. I do not want to be here planning to put her in her final resting place. Life is NOT FAIR. I cried until someone came knocking on the bathroom door, softly asking if I was ok. I'm not.

The Funeral
The morning of the funeral came roaring in, bright-eyed and relentless, oblivious to the weight of the day. Rays of sunlight pierced through the creases of the blackout curtains, stubbornly forcing their way into my room. Why do beautiful, radiant days like these have such a bad reputation? The horrendous images of 9/11 swirl in my mind as I close my eyes, reliving that terrible day for a brief minute. The lush, golden sunshine of that fateful morning was soon swallowed by utter and complete carnage—the dark, heavy smoke from the planes crashing into the buildings wailing across the New York skyline, a stark contrast to the clear blue sky it devoured.

But I digress. *This is the day.* The day when we all have to face the finality of it all. THE FUNERAL. My head feels groggy, pounding like a cook tenderizing meat. I opened my eyes and stared at the ceiling. Thoughts swirled around in my head, a chaotic dance of how to manage the family, how to lead the funeral service, how to survive the day.

BROKEN TO BE RESTORED

SERIES 1

I still can't believe how my mother, brother, and sister were acting towards me.
My-Anne, you must be shaking your head saying girl, how foolish of you, how naïve to expect anything different from the people whose hands are soaked with my blood. Their pride and ego have encapsulated their insensitivity to their part in the family conflicts and the ensuing fall out. But, after today, I will disappear into the dark cloud of My-Anne's passing, hoping never to be found again by these people who call themselves my family.
I swung my feet off the bed. They landed on the floor with a dull thud. Move, feet, move I gently but firmly encouraged them. I have to get ready to put my sister to rest, don't fail me now. It was going to be a long day so there's no time to think. Clothes, food, programs, church contact, funeral home contact—there's too much to do.
The service would be starting promptly at 10 a.m. We were all advised that colored people (CP) time will not be tolerated. All the necessary preparations were already made so just the execution of them remained. My husband of 30 years stood by my side strong and stoic. He has suffered the wrath of my family over the years and has been the blunt of their vindictive tirades. He understood completely how I was feeling so I leaned on him for strength. I admired that without fail he had stepped up his supportive husband's game to see his family through these trying times.
 The pall bearers have arrived. The hearse bearing the coffin was positioned near to the church entrance providing ease of carriage for thepallbearers to bring the coffin into the sanctuary without hindrance.

BROKEN TO BE RESTORED

SERIES 1

It hit me like a ton of bricks as I saw the men lifting the coffin and began to march stoically into the sanctuary. Despite all the drama, grief, it was a wonderful service. Everything went smoothly, there was not a dry eye in the place. You could see and feel the love from many of her coworkers and friends. My-Anne was well loved. I felt like a sleepwalk through it though. I was still so stressed about the falling out of my mother siblings and I. Family fighting over dead left as we say in the islands. It was a hard pill to swallow as I was not trying to fight over My-Anne's dead left property.

The Aftermath
"What shall we say then? Shall we continue in sin that grace may abound? Absolutely not.

But God, I am furious. Furious with my mom, with my siblings, with myself, with the universe itself. At the time our family needed unity the most—during My-Anne's death—my family crumbled under the generational curse of family feuds. They didn't show up. They didn't stand by each other. And instead of owning it, my brother turned the blame on me and my husband. He clung to the idea that we were the ones who failed the family.Deflection at its finest. Why is accountability so impossible for some people? Why do they insist on painting themselves as perpetual victims always the ones wronged, always the 'perfect' ones! It's exhausting. It's infuriating. And it's not the truth.

BROKEN TO BE RESTORED

SERIES 1

We should have been consoling each other and grieving my sister's passing instead we are at each other's throat spitting out years of bottled up slights and resentment. How sad! The past few years replayed in my mind like a scratched record—same scenes, same questions, looping endlessly. I saw us as a family, sitting together, cooking meals, laughing, and sharing moments that felt full of love. But now I wonder, how much of that was real? How much was just a carefully choreographed illusion? Were we only pretending? Pretending to cherish one another. Pretending to forgive. Pretending not to see the fractures forming beneath the surface.

I think of Mom, and sadness swells inside me like a storm tide cresting and propelling itself with fury to crash against the shore. What pain in her past twisted her so sharply against her own children? What betrayal buried itself so deep it turned her love bitter, like floodwaters from the Nile—relentless, drowning every tender thing in its path?

My-Anne and I have asked that question more times than I can count. We searched for clues, yearned to understand her—to unlock the cold silence, to unearth some secret that might make her love us wholly and freely without conditions. Imagine, four children, three girls, two boys clamouring to earn the love of a mother which I seriously don't think we will ever get. My-Anne, you left this world without ever knowing the full, unconditional love of a mother. I carry this ache for you My-Anne.

BROKEN TO BE RESTORED

SERIES 1

For all the answers we deserved but didn't get. And I won't pretend anymore. Not about our family, not about our pain. I'll speak it, write it, and bleed it if I have to— so that your story does not get lost in the silence they still hide behind.
I miss you My-Anne. I miss the you who wasn't afraid to ask the hard questions. The you who was fierce as hell, a bit stubborn, scratch that, a lot stubborn but you meant well. I promise I won't stop asking the hard questions either.
Now it's time for the healing. I feel so broken and fractured like a wounded animal seeking solace knowing its attacker is moving in for the kill. The nursery rhyme of Humpty Dumpty came to mind. It's said that he had a great fall and was broken into many pieces. All the Kings Horses and All the Kings men, could not put Humpty back together again. My exact feelings about our broken family. I know that the scriptures said that God is the God of impossibilities. So, if I fast and pray really hard my family can be put back together again, right? My mother will act right, love her children and grandchildren, and try to stop scamming and scheming to get her way, forgive and forget all who transgressed against her etc, etc. My siblings are the same. Then all will be right with the world. Right?
I feel like I've been to hell and back since her passing. My only consolation prize are my battle wounds which are still so raw it hurts to do anything. Really, really hurts. My children, who were collateral damage in this whole family drama gone awry, made me want to protect their sanity and peace like a fierce mama bear. I am seeking to forge a path forward.

BROKEN TO BE RESTORED
SERIES 1

Lord knows that I just want to write everyone off like a bad debt. But even though it's written off, it never really goes away completely. Does it??

So I will end with this prayer and let go and let God do what he does best. RESTORE what was broken.

BROKEN TO BE RESTORED
SERIES 1

Prayer For Healing

God of the Impossible, I come to you with a heart bruised and cracked, aching with memories and longing for healing. Like a puzzle shattered across generations, my family lies scattered—and I don't know how to gather the pieces. But you do. You see what I cannot. You stitch what no hand can mend.

So I bring you my brokenness. I bring you the bitterness, the silence, the unforgiveness, the betrayal. I bring you the love I still have, even when it hurts to feel it.

Teach me how to pray with courage and wait with grace. Move the hearts of my mother, my siblings, and even my own. Let forgiveness rise like sunlight over a long night. Let peace settle where chaos once ruled. Let love—your kind of love—be louder than resentment.

And even if the miracle doesn't come how I imagined, even if the pieces don't fit the way they once did, help me find beauty in the rebuilding. You are the God who brings life from dust, so breathe into my family. And breathe into me. Take care of My-Anne until the time comes when we will be reunited in heaven. Amen.

LETTER TO MY SISTER/ READER

I know many of you can identify with my story. If we live long enough we will someday lose someone who we really love. Losing a loved one hurts like a Mother. The best way to describe the feeling is that it feels like a part of you was severed off. Yes. Severed, taken off, disconnected. You get it. And, grief is heavy. It rests on your heart like 100 elephants trampling on the tender part.

I can tell you that it will feel less and less heavy with each passing day. I trust God with my grief. I trust him with the fall out with my family. Sometimes, not going to lie, I feel mad at the universe for the grief and pain I was feeling. Do you feel that way sometimes? It's human to lash out especially because pain is unbearable. We are human.

But we are not going to give up, right? Or give in. No! We are going to give God the broken pieces of our hearts and he will, without fail, put them back together again. Trust the process of restoration. It works!

BROKEN TO BE RESTORED
SERIES 1

CHAPTER 7
THE POWER OF PAIN

WRITTEN BY: CAROLYN C. WILLIAMS

"For I know the thoughts I think towards you, saith the Lord, thoughts of peace, and not of evil, to give you an expected end." - Jeremiah 29:11 (KJV)

These profound words from Jeremiah 29:11 have been a constant source of comfort and guidance throughout my journey. As I reflect on the past five years of my life, I am reminded of the unwavering presence of God in every detail of my existence. Despite the highs and lows, the triumphs and tribulations, God has been my faithful companion, my rock, and my ever-present help in times of need.

BROKEN TO BE RESTORED
SERIES 1

My name is Carolyn Williams, and I was born on September 16, 1982. As a single mother of an adult son and two precious grandchildren, I have learned to rely on God's strength and provision in the midst of life's challenges. My heart belongs to the Lord, and I am grateful for the journey that has brought me to this place of surrender and trust.

The year 2020 marked a significant turning point in my life. While the world around me was grappling with the COVID-19 pandemic, I found myself drawn closer to God. The lockdowns and restrictions became an opportunity for me to deepen my relationship with Him, using His Word as a guiding light to navigate the complexities of my soul. Through fervent prayer, fasting, and worship, I began to uncover the layers of hurt and pain that had accumulated over the years.

As I confronted the childhood trauma that had been buried beneath the surface, I experienced a sense of freedom and liberation. The more I surrendered to the Holy Spirit's guidance, the more I felt the weight of offense and unforgiveness lifting off my shoulders. I learned to release those who had hurt me, just as God had instructed me, and to trust in His sovereignty over my life.

However, the journey was not without its challenges. The past two years have been marked by profound grief, as I lost my parents, a sibling, and my beloved Pastor. The pain was overwhelming, and I found myself questioning God's goodness and sovereignty. There were days when I sat in silence, tears streaming down my face, as I cried out to God in desperation.

BROKEN TO BE RESTORED
SERIES 1

Yet, even in the midst of sorrow, I knew that God was with me, holding me close and guiding me through the darkness.

Through this journey, I have come to realize that God's plans for me are indeed good, as promised in Jeremiah 29:11. He has taken the broken pieces of my life and is using them to create a masterpiece of redemption and hope. My story is a testament to the power of God's love and redemption, and I pray that it will encourage others to hold fast to His promises, even in the face of adversity.

As I look back on the journey that has brought me to this place, I am reminded of the importance of trusting God's goodness, even when circumstances seem uncertain. His thoughts towards me are indeed thoughts of peace and not of evil, and I am grateful for the expected end that He has promised me - a future filled with hope, joy, and purpose.

Life has a way of testing our resolve, doesn't it? Broken relationships leave me feeling shattered and alone. Lack of resources made me feel like I was drowning in uncertainty. Ill-health drains my energy and tests my patience. Feeling stuck, with no growth in sight, can be suffocating. Being overlooked and undervalued eroded my sense of self-worth. And then there are the lies, the betrayals, and the continuous disappointments that left me wondering if l will ever find my way again.

But in the midst of all the pain I encountered, something remarkable happened. I discover that pain is not just a passive experience, but a transformative power that shaped me, molded me, and ultimately, set me free.

BROKEN TO BE RESTORED
SERIES 1

The power of pain lies not in its ability to break us, but in its capacity to remake us into stronger, wiser, and more compassionate versions of ourselves.

Pain for me is crucible, a fiery furnace that burns away impurities and reveals my true strength. It was a teacher that guided us through the darkest valleys and led me to the mountaintops of insight and understanding. Pain is a catalyst for growth, pushing me to confront my fears, to re-evaluate my priorities, and to discover new sources of resilience and hope.So, let us not be afraid of pain. Let us not try to avoid it or anesthetize it. Instead, let us face it head-on, with courage and vulnerability. For it is in the depths of pain that we discover the power of our own strength, the depth of our own character, and the boundless potential for growth and transformation that lies within us.

My heart feels like it's been shattered into a million pieces, but I'm slowly gathering the shards and piecing myself back together, stronger and wiser with each passing day.

Bad errors often causes pain for me. By analyzing my mistakes, I identified root causes, understood what went wrong, and developed strategies to prevent future occurrences. This process fosters self-awareness, encourages accountability, and ultimately leads to improved decision-making and performance.

BROKEN TO BE RESTORED
SERIES 1

Here's a breakdown of the key lessons:

- *Understanding the Root Cause:*

Don't just fix the symptoms, address the cause:
When a mistake happens, it's tempting to quickly correct the immediate problem. However, truly learning from it requires understanding why the mistake occurred in the first place.

- *Developing Self-Awareness:*

Identify personal weaknesses and areas for improvement: Errors can highlight areas where you lack knowledge, skills, or experience.

- *Fostering Accountability:*

Take ownership of your mistakes:
Blaming others or making excuses prevents learning. Acknowledge your role in the error and take responsibility.

- *Improving Decision-Making:*

Learn from the consequences of your actions: Mistakes provide valuable feedback on the effectiveness of your choices.

Develop better problem-solving skills: By analyzing mistakes, you can identify patterns and develop strategies for avoiding similar errors in the future.

BROKEN TO BE RESTORED
SERIES 1

Expressions of Pain

The weight of your absence is crushing me; every moment feels like an eternity without you.

- Tears fall like rain, reminding me of the storm that ravaged my heart when you left.
- I'm lost in the darkness of my sorrow, searching for a glimmer of hope to guide me through.

Expressions of Overcoming

- With each step forward, I feel the weight of my heartbreak lifting, and I'm rediscovering the strength I thought was lost.
- I'm learning to love myself again, to find joy in the little things, and to heal the wounds you left behind.
- I'm rising from the ashes, like a phoenix, and I'm determined to make my heart whole again.

Surviving pain can be a transformative experience that fosters growth, resilience, and a deeper understanding of oneself. I survived pain through grace that heaven has afforded me.

BROKEN TO BE RESTORED
SERIES 1

Here are some aspects that can make surviving pain beautiful in the end:

Resilience and Strength
- Developing coping mechanisms: Learning to navigate and manage pain can help build resilience.
- Growing stronger: Overcoming challenges can foster a sense of strength and confidence.

Personal Growth
- Self-discover: Pain can prompt introspection, leading to a deeper understanding of oneself and one's values.
- Newfound appreciation*: Experiencing pain can help appreciate the good things in life and cultivate gratitude.

Empathy And Connection
- Deeper connections: Sharing experiences with others who have faced similar challenges can create strong bonds.
- Increased empathy: Experiencing pain can increase understanding and compassion for others who are struggling.

Appreciation For Life
- Valuing relationships: Pain can help appreciate the importance of relationships and connections.
- Living in the present: Experiencing pain can encourage living in the present moment and appreciating its beauty.

BROKEN TO BE RESTORED
SERIES 1

Beauty In The Brokenness

- Scars as reminders: Scars can serve as reminders of the strength and resilience developed through overcoming pain.
- Growth from adversity: Pain can be a catalyst for growth, leading to a more authentic and meaningful life.

The power of pain is not about being broken; it's about being remade. It's not about being defeated; it's about being transformed. And it's not about being destroyed; it's about being reborn into a stronger, wiser, and more radiant version of ourselves.

Facing continuous pain from a scriptural point of view involves trusting in God's sovereignty and promises of healing and comfort. Here are some recommendations with corresponding Bible verses:

Finding Comfort in God's Presence

- Remember that God is close to the brokenhearted and saves those who are crushed in spirit (Psalm 34:18).

- Trust in God's presence and support, knowing that He takes hold of your right hand and says, Do not fear; I will help you" (Isaiah 41:13).

BROKEN TO BE RESTORED
SERIES 1

Seeking Healing And Restoration

- Claim God's promise of restoration and healing, I will restore you to health and heal your wounds, declares the Lord (Jeremiah 30:17).

- Believe in the power of prayer and the importance of seeking healing through faith, The prayer offered in faith will make the sick person well; the Lord will raise them up. (James 5:15).

Cultivating Resilience And Hope

- Develop perseverance and character through suffering, knowing that "suffering produces perseverance; perseverance, character; and character, hope" (Romans 5:3-4).

- Focus on eternal glory and hope, knowing that "our light and momentary troubles are achieving for us an eternal glory that far outweighs them all" (2 Corinthians 4:17).

Trusting in God's Strength And Provision

- Trust in God's strength and provision, knowing that "the Lord is my strength and my shield; my heart trusts in Him, and He helps me" (Psalm 28:7).

- Claim God's promise of peace and rest, "Come to me, all you who are weary and burdened, and I will give you rest" (Matthew 11:28).

BROKEN TO BE RESTORED
SERIES 1

Finding Peace And Acceptance

- Cast your cares on the Lord and trust in His sovereignty, knowing that He will sustain you and keep you steady (Psalm 55:22).

- Focus on gratitude and trust, cultivating a positive and resilient mindset through scriptures like Psalm 103:2-3, which reminds us to "bless the Lord, O my soul, and not forget not all His benefits, who forgives all your iniquity and heals all your diseases.

As I conclude this journey through the power of pain, it is clear that pain is not just a feeling, but a force that shapes us, transforms us, and ultimately, makes us stronger. Pain is not the end it is the beginning. It's a chance to rise from the ashes, to rebuild, and to rediscover ourselves. Pain is a part of life, but it doesn't define us. We define ourselves by how we respond to pain, by how we grow, and by how we help others. May this book be a reminder that pain is not something to be feared, but something to be learned from. May we rise from the ashes, stronger, wiser, and more compassionate.

One the most important lesson from seasons of pain and the seasons to come is to rely on God through it all, be open to him and lay it all at his feet in total surrender. Surround yourself with like-minded people who has a relationship with God ands can lift you spiritually. It is not God's will for anyone of us to perish but that we may be strong in his might. Pain doesn't have to break you and I, but we can rise mightily and be a light to others who sit in darkness.

Letter To My Sister/Reader

Dear Mary-Jane,

I want you to know, first and foremost, how special you are. And I don't mean it in the way your parents do when they boast about you to their friends and your family, because that always seemed forced, even though I'm sure they meant well.

No, I want you to know how you light up the world with your smile when you show it off. So please, show it off more. I want you to promise me this, even when it gets hard, which I know will and probably still is right now at this moment. You use more of your muscles when you smile, so stretch it out so wide that it hurts and remember when you grow older and see wrinkles around your mouth that you got them from smiling!

I know people are trying to reach out to you to tell you that everything is going to be alright and that they're there for you. Please, and I can't stress this enough, don't push them away or shut them out. You may not want to hear it, but those people are there for you and would do anything to help you.

So, give them a chance even when you don't think they'll understand your pain. You'll never know if you don't let them in. You're feeling alone right now. So alone that you don't think anyone can see the pain you're going through.

I want you to know I see you, okay? I can see the pain written all over your face because I know the look of someone trying so hard to pretend like they're alright when they're crumbling on the inside.

You're not alone, you have people in your life, and even people you didn't see coming, who are more than willing to reach out and be there for you.

I know you feel like you can't get through this. I know it seems like your world is coming down on you and you can't find the strength to get back up. You're spending your days crying in your room, in the shower, while doing laundry, and you can't eat, sleep or find the ambition to go outside and breathe in the fresh air. Do you want to know how I know this? Because I have faced previously. I'm on the verge of tears right now because I went through what is probably the hardest thing I've faced. To be honest with you, I'm barely hanging on by the grace of Almighty God.

I could sit here and tell you in a matter of hours, days and weeks everything will get better. That you will eventually be able to look back at this moment in your life, and maybe even laugh about it. But for those who can't look back yet, that's alright too. I'm on your side. I know I can look back and laugh at what I went through. But I can now look back and tell myself how proud I am for making it through when I wanted to give up.

So, hang in there. You're important to this world and have so much talent and so many ideas to give. You have a light inside you that, if it were to leave this world, there would be a slight darkness that hangs over everyone.

Please. take one day at a time. Everything will eventually fall back into place, so just keep going.

I know you want all the answers now, but I can't give them to you, I can't even give them to myself. I'm with you though, right along the way. We will both get through this.

Sincerely,
Carolyn C. Williams

BROKEN TO BE RESTORED
SERIES 1

CHAPTER 8
BROKEN FRAGMENT

WRITTEN BY: PETRA MITCHELL

The day started like any other day, I was sitting in the living room watching television. The usual routine, Thursday nights at 8pm, I had to watch the Cosby show, having lots of laughs at the Huxtables family or so I thought. I remember my cousin joining in to watch the show and that is the last memory I can recall of that Thursday night.

BROKEN TO BE RESTORED
SERIES 1

I didn't hear anything anyone said to me. My body was sitting there, however I was having an epileptic seizure, not the kind that people are used to, these were the quiet ones, the ones that go unnoticed, undiagnosed and untreated. My unresponsiveness to my cousin's conversation led her to be concerned, which led to me having a discussion with my doctor about the incident. His suggestion was the reason I had to see a neurologist. "Jesus, what is a neurologist"? I said to myself, "there is nothing wrong with my head, the doctors here are always looking to find something wrong, I am as normal as the next person". We did many tests and I was told that I am suffering from what we call "epileptic seizures". What did you say, epileptic seizures? What? no! no! doctor, you got it wrong, please take those tests again.? The doctor's response was: "Petra there is a good chance that these seizures happened before now and no one noticed them, there is a possibility you may grow out of it, however there is no guarantee.

You will have to be placed on medication. My reply was; wait one minute, I am not sick, I don't need any medication, epileptic seizures, you mean Fits, no way!. I am young and healthy. This is a bad joke, a big mistake, a misdiagnosis. I never had fits before, other school children had it, not me, no! no!o. My mind raced, as the doctor continued to ask questions upon questions, for which I had no answers. Petra, are you okay? No, I am still in shock. I know this is difficult for you to hear but look on the bright side, we catch it now and you can be treated with the right medication. My world stopped, medication? . "I will not take it", as the words left my

BROKEN TO BE RESTORED
SERIES 1

mouth. There was a serious look from the doctor and a very serious warning." I know it is a lot being thrown at you, but it is for your safety and health, you must fill and take your medication as prescribed". In that moment my life changed in a dark way, I am only sixteen, just got saved and this is what salvation has brought me. I thought when you become a christian you don't suffer these things, the joke is on me, but I am not laughing. This was not part of my plan for my life, seizure,for the rest of my life?. God you got my name wrong, please check again, there are a lot of Petras, but my first name is not Petra so check your records. This is a nightmare, I will wake up and out of this nightmare. It was like a reality hitting me like a cold winter's day. So I decided to follow the doctor's orders.

Take one dilantin twice per day, one in the morning, one at night. I started taking the medication and boy, I started looking and functioning like a zombie or something out of a movie. I was constantly sleepy and drained. While I was in school, I could hardly stay up, my friend called me the sleeping princess, not knowing I was battling health issues. The dilantin didn't stop the seizures, they got worse and school became a living hell.

The uncertainty of when a seizure can occur put fear into me, so the doctor switched up the dilantin routine. I now felt like a guinea pig , as we worked together to get the right dosage and time to take the dilantin. We continued experimenting hoping to find the right dosage and time to accurately take the dilantin. I am so sick of feeling sick, my bones are sticking out, my collarbone looks like you

BROKEN TO BE RESTORED
SERIES 1

can pour water into it. My weight decreased to under eighty pounds (80). I am dying and no one can help me. This is crazy. Is there a God?
Why now? Why me? There was a storm of emotions inside of me without any warning. I was mad at God, my parents and the dilantin. With this storm came thoughts I never had before, they were dark, like suddenly something entered inside my head and filled my mind with thoughts of death. I tried to ignore the thoughts by praying and reading my bible, well I guess the darkness had found a spot to hide without anyone noticing the subtle changes in me. I started to become introverted slowly that you couldn't tell, withdrawn from social functions and my god, the excuses why I could not meet up with friends or go out to youth gatherings. The voice in my head got louder with each passing day., I smiled and laughed but there was a hurricane hidden behind the smiles and laughter, a pain which had no words to explain. A cry for help that no one heard because it's silent and the mask on my face paints a perfect picture of a young girl saved and happy. I fooled you. The pressure inside my head was real, like that pipe that is about to explode, burst open and what will come out is not peaches and cream. The violent rush of suicide took over my thoughts and the darkness of this formed a laid out plan of execution, this plan would take away the pain of living a life with epileptic seizures, no more dilantin, my mum will not be stressed out and getting calls to come to St Joesph's hospital. I would no longer be a burden to my family, no one would have to pity me or say I am so sorry Petra, you are going through this 'fits things' as the

BROKEN TO BE RESTORED
SERIES 1

Grenadians call it. On this faithful Sunday, after my parents went off to church, I set my suicide plan into motion, I wrote a letter to them explain why I had to leave this world and how it would be easier for them once I am gone. I told my mum that I loved her and that she was an amazing mother and thanks for giving me life, however, this life is wicked to me and that I would be better off dead, than living the life I am given now to live. I emptied the bottle of dilantin in my hands and counted thirty pills. I took a deep breath and swallowed all thirty pills and patiently waited for death to come to have its course with me, ready to leave all the pain and sickness behind. Death didn't come, instead my parents returned from church, found the letter under their bedroom door and rushed into my room. I could hear my mother's voice which seemed far away calling Petra, Petra, wake up, Petra what have you done, don't you know you will go straight to hell, Petra wake up. Something in me wants to wake up but there is something holding my body down like weights. I tried to lift my head but was unable to move. The only way I can describe this is having an outer body experience, I was laying on the bed unable to respond and yet able to somehow step out of my body and see all that was happening around me.

The ambulance came and I heard the paramedics EMS workers calling out my name Petra, Petra, can you tell us what you took. "Madam do you know what medication she is taking and how much is in the bottle", tears fell down my mother's face and my heart ached for the trouble I am allowing my mother to face, because of my stupidity. My inside was screaming for help, mummy I am sorry, I don't

BROKEN TO BE RESTORED
SERIES 1

want to go to hell, I don't want to die, I just want a normal life without sickness, without seizures and medication. A life that does not make me feel like a drug addict, who needs to have her fixed every day for survival, because without the medication what kind of life will I have?. I woke up to see myself at St Joseph's hospital, with tubes in my nose and the feeling of total shame and embarrassment. My system or body had to be flushed out with charcoal. I now had to endure a different type of suffering for my stupid decision. Emotionally, physically, psychologically, and spiritually I was in a battle. Can I be honest? I was mad as hell that I was in the hospital with everyone talking about me. Part of me was happy to be alive and there was a voice in my head I could not shut off. The darkness was still inside of me. They flush out the medication, but couldn't flush out that darkness that was speaking louder than before. I felt alone in the midst of all these people, no one understood my cry, my thoughts, my silence was mistaken for being rude and my frustration was met by giving me medication. I honestly wished I had died at that moment, hell or no hell. I was tired of it all. I was admitted to the hospital for a few days. Let's be real, psychiatric observation is the term. Girl, you have a mental breakdown and you are a child of God, this is not possible. You are saved, going to church, singing in the choir and doing all that good christian young people do but your mind is a hot mess. How is that possible? How can a child of God allow herself to be used by the devil in such a way to bring shame to herself, her family and the church? . The condemnation, I felt in these few days at the hospital, was like gasoline poured out upon a flame of fire already burning at its peak.

BROKEN TO BE RESTORED
SERIES 1

I did not curse or scream. I decided to take it all in and be obedient as a good child would. I promise to get help and that I would never try to commit suicide again. I was released and sent home, with me having cleared with no more suicidal thoughts. Hallelujah thank you Jesus! I returned to school, church and dilantin with a positive attitude, knowing I was given a second chance of life and I am going to make the best of it. Each day I did not have a seizure was a good day, the days I had one was a day from hell. St Joseph's hospital knew my name, like it had become part of their normal routine seeing me every few days as the seizure girl. I was determined to stay on course, with the strategies put in place to help me cope, so I walked, read the bible more, prayed, fasted, stopped wearing perfume and became a little more outgoing. I celebrated my seventeen and eighteen birthday in good spirit, feeling a sense of relief that I have overcome whatever darkness I had faced at sixteen years old.

Yes, I was still having seizures and taking the dilantin but somehow life seemed to have given me a good reason to want to live, oh yes, oh I spoke too soon. One night I decided not to take my medication, since now I was taking two pills at night instead of one twice per day. If you play with fire it's going to burn you. Well, I was about to get burned badly at school. I experienced a seizure that knocked me down from the third floor downwards. It was only God why my neck was not broken or worse..

BROKEN TO BE RESTORED
SERIES 1

So back to the hospital, to be told, Petra why haven't you learned? if stubbornness was an award you would receive it at this point.
Yes, stubbornness and stupidity working hand in hand. Part of me wanted to risk the odds and part wanted just one day without dilantin, to see if or maybe no seizures would occur. I wanted to see if what I was reading in the bible was true. If the God that I gave my life to, can truly heal me. I wanted to prove if all the stories that I was reading in the new testament were true.. I wanted my own encounter, so I tried and failed, however I did not realize trying out this fooliness would open back a very dangerous door that should have remained closed forever. Over a period of time, changes began to take place. At first, it was not noticeable or anything to cause alarm but soon it became apparent that there was a shift in my behavior towards school, and church. I could not focus on my school work and church felt boring, I lost my taste for Friday youth night and let's say Sunday morning was a waste of my time. I did not play with my words or reasons why I don't need to go church on Friday nights and Sunday mornings. If this is what God has to offer me I will pass.,I would rather stay home, sleep, eat pizza and drink coco cola than go to church. I don't like the pastor and these people are getting on my last nerves. There was a ticking time bomb ready to go off. Therefore, I stopped going to church and am now doing my schooling at home with assignments

BROKEN TO BE RESTORED
SERIES 1

from my teachers. I cannot say I missed school. No, it was the best thing for me, I thought, as any seizure I would have, would be at home and not around the whole school for me to feel embarrassed. So with no more in person school and no church, my interaction with people became less and less but that was the trick with the darkness in my thoughts. I totally isolated myself from all contact.
The darkness knew how to make the church feel uncomfortable and point fingers.
Everyday Sunday became a battle of why I do not go around people, I felt one was listening to me, it was my rights and why can't I just be left alone to myself. The voice in my head made it seem that everyone was invading my space and controlling what happens in my life. I started disobeying my mum and not in a disrespectful way , oh it was subtle and smart, oh yes, the darkness was intelligent in the way it gave instructions.
So my relationship with my mum became strained, and the quiet, saved young lady is now talking back and being a smart mouth with her answers.
I did not see the danger and warning signs nor could I recognize them. The voice knew my weakness and it had me, if you want to stop the pain just kill yourself, girl no one will miss you, can't you see they are all better of without you, look how tired you mother is, your father already abandon you long time ago. No one cares if you die. Look not even the church people cares, see no one comes to visit you and they don't call asking about you. No, that's not true.

BROKEN TO BE RESTORED
SERIES 1

They care to laugh more. No one cares or loves you, you have no use. These words rang in my head, especially at nights when I lay down to sleep. My room felt like there was a heavy shadow in the dark, always waiting. "I began to ask myself, if I was going crazy, girl, why would you go crazy"? For people who are old, it's okay to ask a question and I did not answer back myself. Well, the craziness did start, and as the voice filled my thoughts with more darkness, I attempted my second suicide. Yes, you heard me correctly, this well saved christian girl, attempting her second suicide. Oh, yes you will go straight to hell without the hang bag. Girl you let the devil take over.

Why do you want to go down that road again? You did not learn anything from the first attempt. I guess you are one of those who like to feel before you learn. You are so beautiful, but without any sense in your head, I wonder if she is taking any drugs? She is so pretty to be trying to kill herself. Why does my head hurt, my stomach is in knots and why are the lights so bright? .

I asked myself Where am I ? I was told I am in the hospital. Why, I was just at home. , I was asked, Petra, do you know what today is? I replied it was Friday, right?, but I was told Petra today is Monday. The questions kept coming: What's the last thing you can remember? Laying down in my bed and oh! Oh! Petra, why do you want to kill yourself? Don't you think you have a lot to live for? r. The hospital knows my name. We are going through the same routine again, and we are hoping this time you will take the treatment seriously. So I prepared myself to truly get the help that I need to live a normal life.

BROKEN TO BE RESTORED
SERIES 1

It was not easy, trust had been broken, confidence lost and now I had to be supervised daily, like a baby, to ensure I did not harm myself or run away. Once trust is lost it's hard to gain it back. My mum now wanted a step by step breakdown of where I was going, with whom and when I was returning. There were days when I lied about my whereabouts, just so, I did not have to get a lecture on following the rules and there were days when I stayed all day at the library to avoid any form of communication at home.

The saying you can run for so long, however, one day you have to face your problem or demons, well I did not have any interest whatsoever in facing the problem in that moment, I figured if I did not get home when my mum is home, we will not have to speak on the matter of suicide, why do we need to bring up sleeping dogs. The thoughts of having to address these issues started giving me anxiety and made me feel fearful. fear, I love my mum. I promise myself, I will not do anything to hurt her, I have done enough to cause her so much pain and stress.

I continued to play cat and mouse with my mum until my body could not keep up, so it just gave up. I had to face my fears, so I began to open up a little, but I was always looking for any mistakes she would make in her words or attitude which would give me the leverage to stop sharing. The days turned into weeks, weeks turned into months and months into years and I was doing well with a sense of new found hope and the future looked bright. I pressed on still having seizures and taking
medication. I started going back to church, attending the counseling sessions and going to social events,

BROKEN TO BE RESTORED
SERIES 1

trying to make every effort to stay focused and have a positive mind set. I could pretend by telling you right here, that I can do the christian holy dance and tell you that it was all full of sunshine and happy days. I would be a saved liar and I choose to be honest and pray that this honesty will help you. Some days I was not sure if I was coming or going. Some days I laid in my bed and cried and cried to God, cried because I did not truly understand what was happening to me or how to explain it without feeling guilt, shame and condemnation. It is one thing to try suicide, once but not twice. How does a christian get to this point? To me this happens when you feel like there is no one who is listening, everyone is hearing but not listening.

There were days when I was not sure that there was a God or if he was even listening to me, why would he want to anyways, no truly saved christian would try to take their life, not once but twice. I thought about how the rest of my family is feeling, I thought about my siblings, I being the first of eight, what kind of model am I setting for the rest to follow after. The weight of all this hit me like a big stone around my neck, how was I ever going to survive this stupidity?.

The saying "stupid does what stupid think" walked into my head and I somehow started crying and laughing at the same time. I said to myself;" Girl you real dotish, you come all the way to Canada to kill yourself, you real dotish", what you getting on with in them people country?". The tears rolled down my face as a pipe that had been broken and there was no plumber to fix it. I felt a relief that a load had been lifted from me and now

BROKEN TO BE RESTORED
SERIES 1

I can refocus on the journey ahead of me. The years flew by quickly and I was doing well, still having seizures but I am taking my medication and making headway. There is no detour on this road, but there comes the slap in my face, when it rains, it pours, the devils do not play, he is always looking for a way in. Well, let's just say aunty Mary made juice, laced it with alcohol, put it in the fridge and did not say a word to anyone, lord have mercy on me! I came home thirsty and needed to take my medication so I poured it out, took it and drank the juice. Jesus, I need thee. My body went into some strange reaction. I had to call 911, as I had a combination of alcohol and dilantin. If I was not mentally unstable I am about to have an encounter like never before. I remember it like yesterday. My eyes got
bigger, my skin felt weird, my breathing was not right and then I went to lay down, all that I can recall was that I was at the house. I woke up to see myself in the hospital again. St Joseph's nurses and doctors must love me. This time I have no memory of who I am and who is this strange woman in the room with me. You want to guess that it's my mother. Well, I have no memory of her right now, so I am about to scream that there is a strange person in the room and she must leave my room. I watched as the tears ran down her face and her hands reached to touch me, saying, "Petra it is me, your mum" and my mouth, eyes and body say no, you are not and I am scared of my mind. Why am I in the hospital? Father, I promised I would never attempt suicide again,

BROKEN TO BE RESTORED
SERIES 1

I cannot remember what happened. My brain is frozen and not working. I wanted to scream; someone please help me!. I want to go home where my mother is. I screamed mummy, where are you, why am I here? Petra, Petra calm down, please you need to stay calm, my mom replied. . We need to give you some stuff to drink and take some blood, says the doctor. . Why did I ask? The doctors have questions but no one has any answers. My mum was at work and therefore, do not know what happened and I have no memory and cannot give any information.

As the team worked to figure out what caused such a devastating reaction and seizure, the blood work came back. I was then asked, Petra, why did you mix alcohol with your medication, do you understand how dangerous this is for you?At this point I have no answer, because I lost my memory as to what happened. My mind is blank, empty and aunty Mary is not at the hospital to give any answers. The effects of The dilantin and the alcohol had me floating and feeling over elated for a while, then drowsiness hit like a wave from the ocean. I was out, sleeping like a baby.

I was awakened by the loud noise coming from inside the room, these nurses and doctors coming to check in or just down right nosy, whatever the reason was, I did not care, all I wanted was for the noise to stop and my head to stop hammering, so I yelled, can you guys please be quiet, my damned head is splitting open and all you guys are not helping with all these noise. They went completely silent, as if they had a ghost speaking, my eyes popped open looking

SERIES 1

at as if they had a ghost speaking, my eyes popped open looking at
everyone and my mouth opened again saying "mum what are we doing in the hospital", mom looked at me puzzled as to my question. Petra you tried this stuff again, wait, wait, no, no, mum, I came from outside drank juice and took
my medication, oh boy my memory started to come back. What juice ?I did not put juice in the fridge. I replied, well there was juice in there, so I had some with my meds and felt strange, so I called the EMS.
My mum's face turned red and her mouth said something without the words coming out, recognizing that looking like someone is in serious trouble and there will be hell to pay but who I thought would make juice and lace it with alcohol and leave it in the fridge, knowing I could possibly drink from it. The answer to that million dollar question was like lightning, my mind quickly thought of aunty Mary, who was living with us at the time.
Aunty Mary had an alcohol problem and was told before she moved in with us that no alcohol was allowed in the house. I guess aunty forgot about the rules. This horrific experience left me traumatized for a long time.
I had never used alcohol before but I saw the effects it had on family members and individuals and therefore I had vow as a very young child never to mess with alcohol and now someone's action has placed me in physical danger and further psychological stress. The damage had been done and an opening to something even sinister was lurking at the door.

BROKEN TO BE RESTORED
SERIES 1

I started suffering from PTSD, I became afraid to trust people, so I will not drink juice and sleep. I became anxious when going out, especially to events where food and drinks were being served, my mind constantly wondering if alcohol was in any drinks or food and what if I accidentally consumed it again.

These thoughts began to paralyze my daily life and so I retreated back to social isolation, not aware that social isolation can cause depression. I remembered this scripture "For a lack of knowledge my people perish". Yes, I was perishing slowly from the inside out. Lack of appetite took over, I was always sleeping, with no desire for anything. I found excellent reasons for not talking to friends and again not going to church.

I am too fatigued, my clothes did not fit and look at me I look like a dry skeleton with no flesh on my bones. How can my clothes size be O and it's still too big. I was wasting away, my body was rejecting food, like it was a disease. I had to run far away and the seizures were already behaving very badly.

It was as if something gave it permission to move to another dimension in length and occurrences which my petite frame would not tolerate . This was the effects of the concoction of the alcohol and dilantin, the side effects of drug and alcohol poison. Aunty Mary tried her best to apologize for what had happened but I was too weak and furious for any polite conversation, ,so I simply told her that your carelessness and selfishness has caused me more suffering and pain. Why is it so difficult for you not to have alcohol? Why can't you just stop?

BROKEN TO BE RESTORED
SERIES 1

Why is it so difficult for you not to have alcohol? Why can't you just stop? .I wanted her to hurt as badly as I was. The weeks that followed, I chose to stay in my room, avoiding contact with the outside
world as much as possible and sinking more into depression . All you know is that something is wrong but you do not have a name for what it is. I could not even articulate what I was feeling, there were no words to express what my insides were going through. In plain words I was struggling, battling for my life, the taste of something forbidden entered into my thoughts, the darkness, I tried so hard to avoid wanting to make its way back, but with counseling I survived. So with time, I met someone and a relationship started. Oh yes, I am feeling butterflies in my stomach and all the long phone calls made me excited about this new found relationship. I felt like I found someone who cared and loved me even though I had a medical condition.There was peace and safety in the relationship and I navigated through the seizure with new found hope and joy for a year and then the shoes bottom fell off with betrayal. So the safety net I found was gone without warning and I was left confused and angry. How can a person betray someone they claim to love and care about? I was not ready for this life lesson and the pain it caused hurt my heart. Each day I cried and blamed myself for trusting people and letting my guard down. This lesson of love made the seizures function, as if a part of it wanted to take revenge on me for trusting someone,

BROKEN TO BE RESTORED
SERIES 1

so it gave me its own lesson on the TTC bus one winter evening on the way home and so back in the hospital I ended up.. This is where I have to say this seizure was a good thing because it saved my life. At the hospital I was informed that I needed surgery immediately and had it not been for the seizure I could have bled to death.

I gave consent for the operation and it was a success. Now, at home with a broken heart, surgery and seizure, what a mixture of disasters waiting to happen.

You do not give an emotionally wrecked young woman dilantin and pain killers, oh Lord, why put temptation in front of me, when you know I am struggling and the struggle is real. Sometimes I have some good days, other times I have some bad days, when bad days come it is really bad. There was a voice in my head that sounded like a loud speaker, it spoke day and night and I was not able to drown it out or bring it into submission.

The voice would say to me; "why do you think that you can escape, look even your own family wants you dead, the man who left, no one cares, you are no good, no use and definitely God does not love nor care for you, he is the one allowing you to suffer.

As you start believing in him you get sick and all the things in your life are going wrong." " Petra you are a menace to everyone around and yourself. Just do the right thing and end your life. You know what to do: the alcohol and pills work well together, you will not feel any pain no more. Your father already abandoned you and your mum looked at her. She will not care if you die because you will not be suffering anymore." I relapse into my third suicide attempt.

BROKEN TO BE RESTORED
SERIES 1

I locked the bathroom door and began to cry because as I swallowed the combination, my senses came back. I said to myself; what have you done Petra? I called a friend and told her what I did and she called the EMS and I called out to my brother who was sleeping. He was scared and not prepared for this foolishness. He came to Canada to help with my recovery from the surgery, not to see his older sister trying to kill herself. I was rushed into the hospital once again but this time the voice of darkness was with me in the hospital and it made me act crazy in my speech with the doctors and nurses. Once again, I was detoxed or flushed out and got a one way ticket into the psychiatric floor/ward for observation based on my history and what I was saying it called for an alert and staff were concerned about my safety. I was placed into a room by myself and I started begging the doctor to let me go home. I said I will not self harm and I did not want to die, I just want all the pain to stop. The doctor looked at me and said "Petra; . You are in no condition to be released, you need help and we can only help you if you truly decide to let us. I did not have enough strength to fight with the doctor. I remember looking at him and there was something in his eye that said he truly cared about my mental health. This tall Indian doctor spoke with a gentleness and his eyes did not judge me. His next words were "Petra you will be here for the weekend and I will be back on Monday, please take the time to rest and reflect on where you are and what is the next step and also,

BROKEN TO BE RESTORED
SERIES 1

if you could stand and walk without anyone helping you then I will think about letting you go home early but with you coming back once a week for counseling sessions at the hospital and I will be doing blood work." Honestly, I wanted to curse off the man but my body just collapsed into the bed. I don't remember how long I slept for but when I woke up it was midnight and the place was quiet and I was all alone with the bed and walls to face all the demons of hurt, rejection, abandonment, shame, condemnation, and guilt.

The words the doctor had spoken rang in my head over and over. I fell upon my knees and lifted my hands in the air and I began to cry and ask God to forgive me for all the wrongs I had done and I repented and asked God to clean my mind, my thoughts, to take control of my life and make me whole. I had never done anything like this throughout the strugglings. I began to sing the old songs of zion that I remember as they came into my thoughts.

I praised and worshiped the entire night, not even realizing it was morning. The nurse came with a vanilla ensure since I was not able to keep any food down. The doctor had ordered that it be given for meals, after the nurse left I went to sleep for a few hours and got up and went back to praise and worship quoting scriptures I could recall. The weekend passed by without me having any seizures and my body felt stronger than before. The doctor returned on Monday morning, I was able to stand up and was dancing around. g The doctor said to me "Petra what happened? you look different, you are shining, your countenance has changed.

BROKEN TO BE RESTORED
SERIES 1

I responded with Dr. If I tell you, you would not believe me so let us just say a burst of light has shone through over the weekend. I was released from the hospital on Tuesday and attended my counseling sessions for one year without excuses. In my last session the doctor gave me a recommendation to travel to my country of origin to spend quality time with my family, as this would help to strengthen the positive progress that I had made within the year of counseling. I took the advice and stayed with my family for six weeks which gave me peace and clarity for the next phase of my life. I returned to Canada with a deep sense of purpose and devotion to God and my christian walk. I stand tall without shame, guilt and condemnation knowing that my broken fragments have been made whole by God. I am not a victim, I am a survivor,
an overcomer, more than a conqueror through Christ Jesus. What the enemy meant for evil God turned it for his glory. I have been graciously broken to become a vessel of honor. I am in a healthy place psychologically and spiritually.
My last suicide attempt was thirty years ago. I made a choice to stand in the freedom which was given to me by God and never to allow the darkness to enter my space. I now face challenges with faith and hope knowing that my past is behind me, and I have a mandate and purpose to fulfill. The fact that the enemy tried so very hard to kill me, tells me that greatness was inside of me but I did not know that then. . I now understand that no one throws stones or rocks at a tree which does not bear fruit.

BROKEN TO BE RESTORED
SERIES 1

It is pointless. , As I reflect on the stages of my life, I can say after all, I have been through I still got joy, not the joy the world gives but the joy of the Lord which gives me strength to face every day forward with a mindset purged of negative thoughts. Do not get me wrong, I am faced daily with situations, however, I make godly choices which bring about peace. The strategies I learned during my counseling sessions along with fasting, prayer, and mediating upon the word of God help build a young woman, who is not just saved but is in a relationship with her heavenly father. It may sound corny to say but the relationship I have now with God, I did not have then and nor did I have the understanding and wisdom to realize that it takes more than just going to church on Sundays. Having a relationship with God is vital for surviving the attacks of the enemy. Let me be clear: a tree without its root secure into a good foundation cannot stand up
against severe hurricanes. I was a tree without roots and no foundation and so, I got tossed to and fro by the waves. Now as I stand, I do not stand in my own power and strength, for let the weak say I am strong, let the poor say I am rich, for all that he has done for me I give thanks. The road gets rough sometimes and the course of life throws some winter weather but I remain resolute in my commitment to walk the path of light and to let my light shine overtaking the darkness. The only voice I now hear is the voice that makes a difference which is God almighty.

BROKEN TO BE RESTORED
SERIES 1

He has silenced every other voice in my head and gave me a renewed mindset Philippians 2:5. I stand thirty years later to say without a doubt in my mind that I am Petra "I can do all things through Christ who strengthens me Philippians 4:13. This is my anthem as I walk one day at a time allowing the Holy Spirit to take the lead in my life. I once was broken fragments but now I am made whole for His glory. The best is yet to come, do not watch the start but pay attention to the finish.

DEAR SISTERS

I write this letter to encourage you, as you trod the course of your life's journey. The road is not always smooth and straight, it comes with curves and detours along the way, which may lead you to want to give up or find a different path. I am here to encourage you to stay on course. The curves and detours will build your endurance and resilience, as you navigate the path. My beautiful sisters, you are the apple of God's eyes, wonderfully made in his image. I am a living testament that God is able to see you through every storm, hurricane, fire, flood and tsunami. His word declares in Isaiah 43:2 " when you pass through the waters, I God will be with you; and when you pass through the rivers, they will not sweep over you.

When you walk through the fire, you will not be burned; the flames will not set you ablaze." The fact that you are reading this letter now, lets you know that I am still alive and that you can overcome whatever the enemy throws your way. As a young christian back then, I did not understand that I needed a solid foundation to stand upon and therefore the enemy showed up and was able to play with my
emotions for a season but am here to remind you, my sisters every season has an expiry date and so whatever season you may find yourself facing right now it will pass (Ecclesiastes 3:1 states, " To everything there is a season, and a time for every purpose under the heaven." your purpose will break forth. I speak into your lives my sisters grace to persevere, strength for tomorrow and God's love to over shadow every darkness the enemy will send tocloud your mind. For every broken fragments of your life ,there is a potter who specializes in molding

the broken fragments into complete wholeness. It may not look like what you are facing can be made whole my sisters, but God took me out from seizures and suicide and gave me a brand new outlook of life. My mess was not too messy for his outstretched hands. My gorgeous sisters, as I pen this letter to you, I am reminded that it is by the blood of Jesus Christ and my testimony that I was able to overcome my trials. I write unto you without shame, guilt, condemnation and fear knowing that you will be edified, strengthened, encouraged, and motivated to continue in the faith. For the days and nights that you will cry, yell or get angry. I want you to know it is okay to feel the emotions, however, do not give any room for the enemy to take it and use it, be careful to bring every thought into captivity or submission unto the Holy spirit. My strong sisters, see what the Lord has done for my life. It is marvelous in his sight. Broken Fragments chosen for his glory. You made it sisters.

www.ingramcontent.com/pod-product-compliance
Lightning Source LLC
Chambersburg PA
CBHW072150160426
43197CB00012B/2317